SIENA
AND THE HILL TOWNS

With decorations in the text by

JANE GLASFURD

frontispiece The Palazzo Pubblico

SIENA

AND THE HILL TOWNS

ALEC GLASFURD

1962

ERNEST BENN LIMITED · LONDON

First published 1962 by Ernest Benn Limited
Bouverie House · Fleet Street · London · EC4

Printed in Great Britain

TO MY
SIENESE COUSINS

The people here are very ciuil, and euen sociable too; which together with the good ayre, the good exercises for gentlemen, the good language, and the great priuiledges, make many strangers draw bridle here, and sommer it at Siena, the Orleans of Italy.

RICHARD LASSELS [1670]

Cor magis tibi Sena pandit.
[Siena opens her heart to you wider than this]

INSCRIPTION ABOVE THE PORTA CAMOLLIA

Contents

Illustrations

Acknowledgements

THE AUTHOR and publishers wish to thank the following for permission to reproduce their photographs: ALINARI, Florence; ANDERSON, Rome; BIBLIOTHÈQUE NATIONALE (Cabinet des Estampes), Paris; COLOMBINI, Siena; FONTANELLI, San Gimignano; FOTO GRASSI, Siena; the ISTITUTO CENTRALE DEL RESTAURO, Rome; the MANSELL COLLECTION, London (for obtaining the Alinari and Anderson photographs); OMNIAFOTO, Turin; SCALA, Florence; the SOPRINTENDENZA AI MONUMENTI, Siena; and the SOPRINTENDENZA ALLE GALLERIE, Florence.

The provenance of each photograph is indicated in the list of illustrations. Those not specially indicated were taken by the author.

He wishes also to acknowledge his thanks for permission to use quotations from the following books: *Story of Siena*, E. Gardner (J. M. Dent); *The Renaissance in Italy: the Age of the Despots*, J. A. Symonds (John Murray); *Boswell on the Grand Tour: Italy, Corsica and France* (Heinemann and Yale University Press); *Siena and Southern Tuscany*, E. Hutton (Hollis and Carter).

His sincere thanks are also due to many people in Siena, in particular to the Librarian of the Biblioteca degli Intronati for enduring and facilitating his researches, to the Director of the Museo Civico for help in obtaining photographs of frescoes there, to his cousin Dr. Valentino Bruchi for allowing him to borrow from his store of rare books and local knowledge, and above all to Casa Bruchi for its longstanding and unfailing hospitality.

Introduction

SIENA OFFERS the chance to travel in the Middle Ages. Their art, their feeling, and their record surround one. The centre of the town is overwhelmingly fourteenth-century, and this despite many Renaissance and later buildings and the substitution of uninhibited motor traffic for medieval tumults as the murderous element in the streets. Equally important, there has been no drastic uprooting of the community and its traditions either by depopulation or by industry or by war. The railway age left Siena on one side, and did little to disturb the rhythms established during three centuries of gentle dozing under the Grand Duchy. The motor age has reanimated the road on which the town stands, but has fortunately constructed a by-pass and several alternative routes to Rome. Siena, while moving with the times, has thus kept its character as a social unit and escaped becoming a museum in the midst of expanding impermanence. The art of their ancestors means much to the inhabitants; their life is still lived within the framework of the ancient wards or *contrade*; people speak of St. Catherine as if she had died almost within living memory; and the *palio*, though not strictly a lineal descendant of the horse-race first mentioned in 1238, has provided excitement for many generations of townsfolk and is only incidentally a show for tourists.

Today Siena is the equivalent of a county town, with a university, an excellent academy of music, various small industries and trades, and busy agricultural market. It is a city of contrasting moods. The tall, pavementless canyons with their groups of loiterers strike a rather sombre note, but that only serves to enhance the surprise of the sunlit piazzas. At evening one can pause outside the Porta San Marco to look out over the dim waves of the Tuscan countryside and hear the gentle melancholy of the bells—for Siena, like Oxford, is a city of bells—but on returning to the centre one is immediately plunged into that vigorous collective phenomenon the *passeggiata*, and can study the unending interplay of self-consciousness, social aspiration, and courtship, cleft at intervals by virtuoso performances on such percussion instruments as the Vespa. Siena is still very much alive.

Paradoxically this modern Italian small-town throng contributes to the overmastering sense of the past, partly because one sees the same faces as in late medieval frescoes, and also because the Middle Ages were full of vitality and noise, ferment, sudden emotions, and display. It is suburbia that kills the medieval, and Siena is not suburban.

The high-piled town of old rosy brick and cold stone straggles along the crests of three ridges, set star-shaped with lesser tentacles, each of them reaching out to a gate in the fourteenth-century walls. These walls, a complete girdle whose outline bears some slight resemblance to the map of England and Wales, run sharply uphill and downhill in places in order to enclose the upper ends of several short, deep valleys, two of them densely built over, the others a tangle of orchards, vineyards, and allotments. By the star's centre, just off the crest where the three main streets and their traffic impetuously meet, hangs the great scallop-shaped piazza, the Campo, with the magnificent city hall along its lower edge and the giant bell-tower bursting rocket-like into the sky. Not far away, on the highest point of all, the cathedral stretches its tiger-striped length. The severe palaces of the aristocracy line these central streets and, farther out, bastions and gaunt churches overhang the escarpments that fall away on both sides. [*Plate* 1.]

Siena is one of the few places left where, with comparatively little effort, one can step back six centuries and meet the medieval inhabitants. No other town that I know conveys so much of the true feeling of the Middle Ages, stripped of their sentimental ivy. To this impression the austere power and religious emotion of Sienese painting contribute much, as does the functional ensemble of Gothic buildings on a knot of hills. These pictures and streets reflect a strong, fascinating collective personality, that of the Sienese commune. What one should look for in Siena is less the individual works of art, fine as they are, than the way in which they hang together and reveal the thoughts of the people who made them. As a matter of fact Siena possesses only one piece of architecture that is unchallengably at the top of its class, namely the tower of the city hall. But what gives Siena an almost unique interest among Italian towns is the legacy of its remarkable life as a free city-state. For four centuries, from the early Middle Ages until the close of the Renaissance, this was a fiercely independent commune with its own coinage, economy, and civilization, its own curiously isolated school of painting, its own ebullient political life which was the most vigorous in Italy and the least understood by outsiders. Long after every other town had succumbed to some variant of dynastic or oligarchic rule, or had been swallowed up by some larger neighbour, the Sienese were still in love with freedom and political justice. Although they pursued those elusive but essential values with more zeal than discretion or success, they resisted the trend to tyranny for longer than anyone else, and that, with their art, is their chief claim to our attention.

In Siena therefore, more than elsewhere, history is the key, and even a moderate acquaintance with it brings the place to life as nothing else does. Many of us at least will find the story of this brave, wayward, gifted people and the ups and downs of their free city easier to follow than the strange and remote language of their painting. The Sienese, like the Greeks, were forerunners, and the things they achieved and quarrelled over are, in essentials, the same as those that concern us today. I have accordingly tried to sketch Siena's history with rather more detail than is usual in travel books, and to compensate for this by commending rather fewer religious pictures to a reader whose sustained enthusiasm for this genre is likely to fall short of what some writers seem to assume. Sienese pictures are exquisite, and some of them immediately enlarge one's sense of beauty, but they are too sacred and too many. The non-specialist will get most from a highly selective approach. Even so, the newcomer to Siena should be warned that these feline Madonnas, and the early ones in particular, are a taste that rapidly grows on one.

Sienese history, though having the intimacy and charm proper to the life of a small community, is by no means parochial. It is involved in important movements, and the horizon is European. I have been intrigued to find almost as many links with Scotland as with any other country. The chief one is provided by that most Italian blend of adaptability and principle, Pope Pius II. I confess I have found it less easy to sympathize with the public life of the extraordinary woman he canonized, St. Catherine of Siena. The saint and the pope are the two poles of Sienese life; she made no concessions whatever to the age she lived in, and he made rather too many to his. Our own age, which tries to be a humanist one, will prefer his fault to hers. But no age, of course, can judge St. Catherine except by standards other than her own.

From the time when I first stayed here as a small boy I have been fascinated. Except for more traffic and some tolerably well-planned housing estates at various points outside the walls, it has not changed much. The second war saw British tanks rocking perilously through the narrow streets, but apart from the bomb-hits on the Osservanza very little damage was done. The upper class still lives in an atmosphere that seems a little heavy to onlookers, but which is redeemed by the bonds of genuine mutual affection within their large households. The middle class has grown greatly in size and prosperity. The workers are still for the most part craftsmen; there is still a street devoted almost exclusively to coffin-making where from each doorway the rich old ladies are quietly appraised as they pass. They still mend the roads by chiselling an alarming hail of chips from the tyre-polished surface of the flagstones so as to give a better grip. Visitors fortunate enough to have teeth as sound as those of most Italians will enjoy *panforte*, a glorious dense sugary slab of nuts and candied peel that has been the pride of confectioners here since the thirteenth century. Another culinary masterpiece is *pollo alla creta*, chicken baked inside a clay envelope which keeps in the savour. Then there are the little hill towns of the district to explore. San Gimignano is well known, but there are many others—early-Renaissance Pienza, late-Renaissance Montepulciano, Poggibonsi of the fat straw-covered bottles, medieval Massa and tower-encircled Monteriggioni, Montalcino and Radicófani, with country houses, abbeys, and ancient fortified villages in profusion. And all around for a score of miles are the pale Tuscan hills, olive-clothed to the north and bare to the south, ploughed by slow white oxen and punctuated with cypresses, a clean, classic landscape that, like the Tuscan speech, is the most perfect in Italy.

Tethering-rings, Porta Romana

1

Early Medieval Siena as it was

IN THE YEAR 711, the thick haze that obscures Siena in the Dark Ages lifts abruptly to reveal two groups of men standing in front of a small country church and arguing volubly about a saint's bones. On the one side are the *gastald* or governor, the judge, and the bishop; the two laymen have Lombard names and the latter two are related. On the other side is the bishop of Arezzo, the uncertain boundary of whose diocese extends, so he claims, to within sight of Siena. This alien prelate and his entourage have been caught in the act of sneaking off with the body of St. Ansanus, a locally much venerated martyr who, some four centuries earlier, was beheaded by the Romans after his sanctity had preserved him from being satisfactorily *sauté* in boiling oil. Rather than let Arezzo have their saint, the entire population of Siena rushes down from their neighbouring hilltop, interrupts the discussion, drives off the opposing bishop and his men, and forcibly shifts the diocesan boundary to a more decent distance.

With this incident Sienese history is born. Everything about it is typical of what comes later—the cousinship of the leading characters, the unassimilated aristocracy, the ecclesiastical tangle, the sudden universal spurt of public energy when the community's honour is seen to be threatened from outside. Nor did the affair end there. With the litigious pertinacity of simple folk, this issue was keenly contested in all possible courts for four hundred years, when the dispute ended in a rather gruesome division of the spoils.

Siena is much older than its written history. Probably the hill where the cathedral now stands was never without a settlement of sorts. The enigmatic Etruscans left behind a few tombs for certain, perhaps the name Siena, and just conceivably their artistic talents in a kind of historical cold-storage. Of the small Roman township founded by Augustus, mentioned in one of Tacitus' anecdotes and evangelized by the uncookable St. Ansanus, virtually nothing remains; its street-plan is uncertain and its municipal institutions did not survive the Dark Ages. Only the lean she-wolf suckling the twins, a civic emblem from very early times, testifies to some awareness of a Roman past. We may safely reject the malicious etymology of the Florentine chronicler Villani, who ascribes the founding of this rival city to some camp-followers left behind by Charles

Martel—'all the old men and those who were sickly and could not bear arms'—the place being called Sena because they were senile. There was a bishopric from about the year 650, if not before, though again we need not follow Villani, who says it was established through the influence of a travelling cardinal who wished to do his Sienese landlady a favour. As for civil authority, the garbled records tell of the coming and going of shaggy Lombard *gastalds* and uncouth Carolingian counts, who exercised whatever higher jurisdiction there was, but their power waned and by the eleventh century the local landowners were practically a law unto themselves.

Such unrestricted feudalism was, in fact, a fertile soil for the seeds of urban society. The medieval town started life as a legal and social anomaly, a republican acorn in a feudal cornfield. By a series of privileges and exemptions it gradually escaped from the control of its immediate overlord. Siena, like some other Italian towns, was built on land originally owned by a bishop. His temporal power was relatively easy to demolish. But complete communal freedom was only possible in an area where the monarchy ruled, at most, intermittently—which was exactly what was then happening in all these lands between Rome and the Alps, nominally subject to the Holy Roman Empire, but in fact usually a power vacuum.

Another precondition of freedom, a strong economy, was less easily satisfied. Siena stands where an ancient north-to-south road, known as the Via Francigena or nowadays, incorrectly, as the Via Cassia,* crosses the watershed between several small, unnavigable rivers. The immediate neighbourhood is not rich farming country like the great strath of the Arno and the supply of water is not unlimited. A short distance to the west, rough untamed hills bar the nearest way to the sea. To the south the well-known reddish soil quickly fades into the bleak, off-white clay scarps often seen in the background of Sienese paintings. Northwards rise the Chianti hills, less favoured then than now. The site has more military than economic virtues, and it was clearly not geographic destiny that transformed a convenient staging-point on the road to Rome into a city-state that rivalled Florence.

The motive force was, in fact, banking. About the year 1200, or even earlier, the leading families of this upland town followed the example of the more famous merchants of Lombardy and set up business as bankers. At that time patterns of social behaviour had not hardened and these *gentiluomini* or *grandi*, while keeping their landed estates and investing some of their commercial profits in them, showed no aristocratic misgivings about engaging in trade. They soon discovered that dealings in foreign exchange were more profitable than financing the modest local economy. In countries without banks they became the bankers, and as such they regularly attended the great fairs in north-eastern France and elsewhere, changing and lending money at the extremely high rates which the many risks and the absence of an easily enforcible commercial code might justify. True, the Church forbade usury, austerely defined as lending money for interest, and the recent Lateran Council of 1179 had renewed this prohibition. But Sienese

* The classical Via Cassia ran thirty miles farther to the east, through the Val di Chiana. Its use in the Middle Ages was impaired by floods.

bankers, useful people, were able to produce letters from the pope himself threatening spiritual penalties to such as refused to pay their debts, and in time practice changed theory—it is long since the Italian hierarchy can be accused of anti-capitalist prejudice.

With papal backing and patronage, the financiers of Siena had disproportionate success. Soon they were much engaged in collecting papal dues abroad, advancing money at suitable rates of interest to those newly-preferred prelates who had to pay them, and transmitting the proceeds, less commission, to Rome. By being good at their job some of them achieved unpopularity as far away as England, where their presence is first deplored in 1229.

Even the beginnings of activities like these increased the town's importance and launched it on a political career. By 1125, if not sooner, there was a municipality headed by *boni homines* and annually elected consuls. There is no record of any foundation charter and their authority seems to have been usurped from the shadowy count, of whom little more is heard, and from the bishop, who was expelled at one time after he had rashly quarrelled with and excommunicated the consuls. The town now began a long struggle to extend its control over the surrounding district. One by one the outlying feudal lords were induced or forced to submit to the town's jurisdiction and to reside within its walls for so many months each year, or at least to make binding treaties of alliance. All this lacked legal sanction and was against the policy of the emperor. For the moment Frederick Barbarossa was heavily and unsuccessfully engaged in war with the Lombard League of cities, who had done the same things a few decades earlier. In 1179 his legate, in return for protestations of loyalty and a money consideration, was glad enough to grant the Sienese a charter recognizing their rule over such parts of the county or *contado* as they had already acquired. But in 1186 the imperial army arrived in Tuscany to suppress the communes' independence and restore the feudal order. Siena, though Ghibelline or imperialist in ideological allegiance, followed a Guelf policy in practice and stood a siege rather than submit. It would probably have been a Guelf city outright if Florence, already a dangerous rival, had not upheld that cause.

The great fault of the Middle Ages was to attempt vast tasks with ridiculously slender resources—to try to understand the universe with the aid of an incomplete edition of Aristotle, to conquer and hold large areas of the Middle East with a few thousand front-line troops or, in the case of the Holy Roman Empire, to govern half Europe with a revenue, civil service, and army that did not suffice to manage southern Germany. The trouble was that the extraordinary dynamism of these enterprises usually carried them far enough to bedevil more feasible ventures. In Italy and Germany peace, the advancement of civilization, and national unity were sacrificed to the mirage of a secular counterpart of the papacy, a concept to whose realization the papacy itself was hostile. In practice the emperors relied for support on the principle of feudal allegiance, that is on social elements that, in most of Italy, were already on their way to being superseded by an urban bourgeoisie. No north Italian town could be wholeheartedly on the side of the Empire for its own sake, when the Empire's complete victory would have meant setting bounds to the town's self-government and expansion. Those towns such as Siena which were Ghibelline were so by compulsion, or for what they could get out of it; they hoped to hold the balance against rival towns which were Guelf, and to gain the help of imperial armies and of the malcontent nobles in revolt against neighbouring city-states.

The siege of 1186 ended in a compromise. An imperial charter recognized the consuls' authority as legitimate, but freed the territorial barons from their control. The bishop paid the penalty for being a genuine Guelf by having his lands put under the consuls' jurisdiction. The town was granted the right to coin money and to tax its citizens. Eleven years later, with the next temporary collapse of the Empire's power, the Sienese promptly started reimposing their rule over the lordlings around them, and this time the clock was not put back again.

Siena was by now an effectively independent city-state, and celebrated the newly assured status by a reform of the executive. A single official, the *podestà*, replaced the consuls. His jealously circumscribed term of office lasted twelve months, and for fear of corruption or subversion he was usually chosen from a distant town. Even these precautions were not enough; in 1240 the *podestà* led an aristocratic rebellion against a recently broadened magistracy and, after his defeat, subsequent holders of the office had their political powers reduced; by the end of the century the *podestà* had been transformed into the senior judge.

A more important consequence of statehood was the almost immediate birth of party politics. From now until the extinction of independence in the sixteenth century, party strife was meat and drink to the Sienese. Other cities succumbed fairly soon to despots, dynasties, or long periods of domestic apathy; not so Siena. It has been usual for historians to deplore these factions and for the layman to tire of them, but these attitudes show a lofty or lazy contempt for the plain fact that party politics are the index of a free state's vitality. At least it can safely be asserted that no other medieval Italian people led so full a political life for so long as the supposedly soft Sienese, a point which has often been successfully concealed by the genius and patriotism of Florentine historians.

Sienese parties or *monti* had a class, almost a caste basis. Membership of a party tended to be hereditary rather than a matter of personal choice. We hear of the first crisis in 1212, when St. Francis of Assisi came to mediate between the *grandi* and the *popolo*. The latter owed their organization not, as in other cities, to the guilds, but to the militia, of which they were the infantry element. By 1233 the *popolo* had grown strong enough to insist on sharing power. The government became a council of Twenty-Four, with its membership at first equally divided between the two parties. The *capitano del popolo*, by origin the elected leader of the commons, soon became a great officer of state second only to the *podestà*. In 1262 there was a written constitution worthy of the Abbé Siéyès, laying down rules for the four *provveditori di biccherna* or lords of the treasury, for their secretary the *camarlingo* (usually a mathematically gifted monk from the abbey of San Galgano), for various *balìe* or committees, including the Thirteen Amenders charged with revision of the statutes, for the revenue, military conscription and various public services, and for tightening the screws on the unfortunate *podestà*; the law even prescribed the guests allowed at his dinner-table, and his bedtime. There was also a *parlamento* or assembly of all citizens, but the name is misleading; it was seldom summoned and was never a deliberative body. What we should call the parliament or legislature was the Council of the Bell, with three hundred members. It decided all major issues, voted taxation, and appointed officials. A constitution as advanced in its way as Britain's before the Reform Bill, always remembering that in both cases most of the inhabitants were not enfranchised.

In trying to find one's way through the bewildering internal history of Siena it is helpful to realize that all elections took place within parties and within wards. The proportion of seats or places in the government allocated to parties changed fairly often, but there were always three equal major wards or *terzi* corresponding to the three steep ridges on which Siena is built. For this reason the number of councillors, whether the Twenty-Four described above or of later councils such as the Thirty-Six, the Nine, the Twelve, and the Fifteen, was always a multiple of three, and also bore a relation to the party proportion of the day.

While these matters were being settled, Siena had embarked on an adventurous foreign policy. Like Florence at that time and many aspiring powers since, the Sienese state was landlocked and tried hard to find a way to the sea. The only direction open was to the south-west, fifty miles down the Merse and Ombrone valleys. This meant having to subdue other towns as well as recalcitrant barons. Some small places like Montalcino and San Quirico were taken without much difficulty, and in 1224 a more ambitious expedition captured Grosseto. 'Never was there seen a fairer host,' say the Sienese chroniclers. 'Their shields, their armour and their tents lent such splendour to the country round about that it seemed another paradise.' . . . 'And on their return, for joy at that victory, there was great feasting with many bonfires, and all the shops around the Campo were closed.'

This campaign won for Siena a foothold on the coastal plain of the Maremma, a desolate countryside of swamps and great white oxen. But Grosseto lies some miles inland and the Sienese had yet to get their seaport. Nor did the powerful Counts Aldobrandeschi take kindly to their presence there. One of them refused to yield even when his castle walls were stormed. 'He rode round the castle yard like a dragon,' we are told, killing many of his foes, until some conscripted townsman 'struck him with a mace of iron upon his head, and so caused him to quit this world'.

In their drive towards the sea the Sienese were taking a calculated risk, for in the opposite direction, at one point a bare six miles from the city, lay the long-disputed frontier with Florence. This power, the strongest in Tuscany, disliked Siena's expansion. The years after the capture of Grosseto saw Florentine armies twice encamped before Siena's northern gate. Being unable to get any further, they contented themselves after the fashion of the time with insulting behaviour; a Florentine hero hung his shield on the gate and dead donkeys were catapulted over the walls, for, as a medieval Clausewitz writes in advocating the latter measure: 'Though it will not harm the enemy it will make him dislike himself with annoyance.' In these campaigns the boundaries of the *contado* swelled and shrank, minor towns like Montalcino and Montepulciano were taken and lost again, and at a low ebb in Siena's fortunes there was even a one-sided treaty of everlasting peace which was not broken for three years. Then, encouraged by imperial victories in the far south and by the philippics of Provenzano Salvani, the leading Sienese Ghibelline, at home, Siena gave shelter to some Florentine rebels and so provoked the War of Montaperti.

Ardent histories of Siena are wont to dwell on this epic campaign at disproportionate length, but as it brought more glory than long-term profit we may at least pass over the preliminary manoeuvres, both political and military, and reach the critical moment when the largest army which Florence had yet put into the field came clattering down out of the Chianti hills and encamped beside the road to Arezzo, within sight of the city's towers and just beyond the little river Arbia. The Florentines brought with them some contingents of not altogether dependable allies and their own *carroccio*, a great four-wheeled, vermilion-painted, ox-drawn waggon fitted with twin masts from which flew the white-and-red banner of their commune. With it was another waggon carrying a heavy bell that was rung by hammers at appropriate moments, which, given the commanding officer's self-importance and the Latin attitude to noise, one may assume meant more or less continuously. Sending envoys to demand surrender in peremptory terms, the Florentines sat down and waited for fear and treason to work in their favour.

The Twenty-Four rejected the summons and, rather than face a siege, prepared to march out to battle. They had with them the imperial vicar and 800 German heavy cavalry who, once they had received double pay, were full of the right spirit; there were also the Ghibelline exiles from Florence and allied knights from the *contado*. All these mounted allies could be employed better in the open country than behind the city walls. The citizen army, numerically much larger but mostly infantry, was organized in three divisions like everything else Sienese. In the absence of the *podestà*, who it appears was still besieging Montalcino with a small force, one Buonaguida Lucari was elected political leader with full powers. He had the inspiration to lead a penitential procession to the cathedral and to dedicate the hard-pressed city to the Virgin in a moving and sincere act in which the whole city took part.

Next morning, with morale and banners high, the army marched out of the Porta Pispini, but what with protracted *chants du départ* and thirteenth-century staff-work it took them most of that day to get into position on a ridge less than three miles distant, and there they spent the night.

After a substantial breakfast—'Q' was evidently better than 'G', as in most democratic armies—the Sienese and their allies crossed the Arbia and delivered a frontal attack, while a detachment moved far round the enemy's left flank, behind a hill, and just at the critical moment charged down from the rear. Then came

lo strazio e il grande scempio
*che fece l'Arbia colorata in rosso;**

* 'The havoc and the great slaughter that dyed the Arbia red' (*Inferno*, 10, 85–86).

but neither Dante nor modern translations of *La Sconfitta di Montaperti* convey the crude metallic slogging-match that was the crux of medieval war as well as Barbour's description of a battle of fifty years later which saved another small country and reddened another stream:

With all thar mycht and all thar mayne
Thai layd on, as men out of wit;
And quhar thai with full strak mycht hit
Thar mycht no armyng stynt thar strak;

. . . . .

So gret dynnyng ther wes of dyntis,
As wapnys apon armor styntis,
And of speris so gret bristing,
And sic thrawing and sic thristing,
Sic gyrning, granyng, and so gret
A noyis,——

Finally the chivalry of Florence had had enough, and set spurs to their horses; in retrospect they blamed a certain Bocca degli Abati for the fall of their standard, and the real or supposed treason of one saved the faces of many. The foot-soldiers, thus abandoned, fought bravely but were slaughtered wholesale, the *carroccio* and much booty were taken, and a remnant was allowed to surrender at nightfall on the knowe of Montaperti.

Dante, when he met Bocca degli Abati in the lowest regions of hell, forgot his own treasonable expectations from foreign princes and patriotically added to the wretch's torments. (*Inferno*, 32, 76 ff.)

Siena had been saved. Indeed for a short time our city dominated Tuscany. A deputation from rebellious Montalcino, appearing with ropes round their necks like the Burghers of Calais, was made to bury the dead. The northern frontier was pushed back beyond Poggibonsi. The imperialists entered Florence, and would have razed it to the ground but for the stand taken by Farinata degli Uberti, a Florentine rebel baron who had helped to rout his own countrymen. He 'openly forbade the deed', and the other Ghibellines were overawed by this indomitable exile, who afterwards* could raise himself out of the flames of hell to correct Dante with a gesture of contempt for his surroundings—*come avesse lo inferno in gran dispitto.*

Montepulciano was reduced once more, and Provenzano Salvani went to build a castle intended to dominate the place in future. Radicófani, still further south, was taken from the pope. But this Indian summer of the Ghibellines lasted little more than five years. Then the imperial army was overthrown in the titanic battle of Benevento, in the far south; and, though Siena welcomed the young prince Conradin on his way towards Rome with a forlorn hope, and the Holy Father peeped anxiously over the battlements

* *Inferno*, 10, 36.

of Viterbo as his enemies passed by, the news of a thirteenth-century Culloden soon rang the death-knell of an old-fashioned cause. The Guelfs returned to Florence, and the great Provenzano held a beggar's bowl in the Campo until he had collected enough to ransom a friend.* A few months later he himself was taken prisoner and beheaded after a locally decisive defeat at Colle di Val d'Elsa. Siena, making the best of a bad business, re-admitted her Guelf exiles and expelled a few of her Ghibellines, changed the ruling Twenty-Four into Thirty-Six (in which only 'good merchants of the Guelf party' might sit), joined the league of cities led by Florence, and in short accepted a sensible settlement instead of extinction. The Sienese Wolf and the Florentine Lion shook hands, a little reluctantly, as we see them doing in one of Neroccio's graffiti on the cathedral pavement. As the dust subsided, the outlines of a new and greater age became visible.

* *Purgatorio*, II, 133–138.

2

Early Medieval Siena as it is

IT TAKES SEVERAL generations to evolve a local style of architecture. The great Gothic palaces that are the city's glory were derived from cruder buildings which met the needs of a simpler society. Quite a lot of this rudimentary Siena can be found today in odd corners, though it is often overlooked. The search for it shows how a frightened huddle of private blockhouses began to grow into a highly organized commercial and artistic community. It also reveals, among other unexpected things, the origin of the distinctive Sienese arch.

The oldest part of the town is, obviously enough, the highest part, that is the short ridge running south-west from the Duomo. On the latter's site stood its rude predecessors, now gone without trace. At the other end of the ridge, some five hundred yards away, was the castle of the counts, in what is now a poor area of abrupt dead ends and twisting alleys, one of which is still called the Via del Castelvecchio, although the old castle itself disappeared at a very early stage. A small, ancient tower, La Rochetta, is said to be a vestige of it. Next door the little church of Sant' Ansano, named after the first of Siena's coruscation of saints, dates back to the ninth century but has been drastically restored inside. The whole of this south-western hill, being the original nucleus, is called the Terzo di Città; the twelfth-century extensions along the ridges northwards and south-eastwards are the Terzo di Camollía and the Terzo di San Martino respectively. [*Plate* 2.]

When the emperor's German troops besieged the town in 1186 they did not attack the present ramparts, but a much smaller circuit of walls. This inner ring can still be traced in places, often only by the alignment of streets, running roughly round or just inside the edge of the present built-up area, but excluding the long tentacles which stretch out towards the later gates. Several gateways of the earliest circuit remain round the Terzo di Città, engulfed amid taller buildings, and there is another one, belonging to an intermediate extension of the walls, at the far end of the Via di Pantaneto.

Within these walls the thin fortified towers of the *grandi* stood up, as we are told by one who saw them, like a thicket of canes. To get an idea of what the skyline of Siena looked like even as late as the time of the French Revolution, one must go to San Gimignano. In the thirteenth century Siena had well over a hundred of these towers, and they did not begin to disappear until about 1550, when the Spanish garrison used some as quarries for stone to build their fortress. Most of the rest were cut short or demolished after an earthquake in 1798. A number of these family towers can be found embedded in later buildings in the central streets. For instance, there is one at the Croce di Travaglio, another in the Banchi di Sotto, two others at the southern end of the Via dei Montanini, yet another at the far end of the Via di Città, while the huge tower of the Ballati family still sticks up out of the buildings behind the Piazza dell' Indipendenza and is a prominent object on the skyline.

The leading families built round a small courtyard, surrounded by a defensive wall and with one or more towers attached. What is left of one of these *castellari*, with courtyard, tower, and entrances, stands opposite the church of San Vigilio not far from the central crossroads, though it scarcely repays the trouble of finding it. Such private forts and towers stood on high ground, while the dwellings of lesser folk, constructed mainly of timber in that early period, squeezed in between them or spread down the slopes towards the perimeter.

With the growth of trade and banking during the thirteenth century, houses began to be built on less military lines. The easiest way to see what happened is to start from the far end of the Via di Città, which is the left-hand or western arm of the 'Y' formed by the three main streets at the centre. There, on the corner of the little Piazza Postierla, stands the uncompromising fortress-tower of the Forteguerri, in which everything has been sacrificed to military considerations and there are virtually no ancient openings at all. To see the next stage in the evolution of domestic comfort one crosses the piazza and walks a few yards up the Via Stalloreggi. On the right-hand side of the street, just past the defaced remnants of another tower, is a good example of a *casa-torre*, at the time of writing numbered 14/16, and dating from round about 1230 or 1240. On the ground floor are two openings with pointed arches, close together and very tall in relation to their width. Some twenty-five feet above the street level appears a pair of Gothic windows, each divided by a column. These windows are simple but decorative, a great addition to the lighting and amenities of the best room, and there is another pair on the floor above. The starkness has gone; it is a house built in the form of a tower. [*Plate* 4.]

Still further up the street, on the other side, we come to the battered but still recognizable Palazzo Bisdomini, in which the basic elements of the *casa-torre* have been expanded laterally so as to form the façade of one of the earliest surviving palaces. The street ends at the Porta Stalloreggi or Arco delle Due Porte, originally a double gateway as can be seen from outside, and the best preserved opening in the original circuit of walls. The small house just before it on the left belonged to the painter Duccio, though it has suffered many changes since his time.

The Via Stalloreggi is an interesting street, well worth a brief exploration. Among its attractions is the shrine of the Madonna del Corvo, high up on an angle past the Palazzo Bisdomini. Here, legend has it, a carrion crow fell dead in the spring of 1348, infecting those who touched it and thus introducing the great plague of that year—a legend no doubt encouraged by all commercial travellers who had returned to Siena after passing through the plague centres of Genoa and Pisa.

The Albergo Toscana in the Via Cecco Angiolieri (formerly the Via del Re) is another excellent example of a Sienese palace of the mid-thirteenth century. It was once the Palazzo Rinuccini. The construction is peculiar, for the top floors rest on stilts, great pillars of masonry nearly twenty-five feet high, the narrow spaces between them being partly filled in with lighter work. It appears that this kind of construction was copied from Pisa, where the weight of the house had to be supported on clusters of piles driven deep into the soft soil at intervals. Rising on these foundations, the pillars are linked at the top with pointed arches to frame the windows on the *piano nobile* and take the thrust of the upper storeys. On the other hand depressed round arches, or even in some cases horizontal lintels, suffice to carry any sections of infilling between the pillars. Siena is built on hills of solid sandstone, and the Pisan stilted construction was soon modified and then abandoned altogether. But the combination of a depressed round arch below a tall pointed one was retained and, when the two arches were brought together so that they sprang from the same level, there was born the typical Sienese arch, as seen on the ground floors of innumerable medieval buildings and the Palazzo Pubblico in particular.* [*Plates* 4, 28, *and* 29.]

Almost opposite the Albergo Toscana is another old house, smaller and of much less architectural interest, but worth a glance for its literary connexions. It is the Casa Angiolieri. A contemporary inscription on the wall states that its owner began to build it in 1234 when he was banker to Pope Gregory IX, doubtless a profitable line of business. His grandson was the bohemian poet Cecco Angiolieri, the black sheep of his douce, strait-laced family, who would have been horrified to see the street recently re-named after him. Another link with Cecco, of whom we shall hear more presently, is a contemporary memorial stone to his eldest son Deo, to be found close by in an attractive small cloister behind the church of San Cristoforo, on the outside of the apse.

Once one knows what to look for, one is continually finding traces of *case-torri*, Pisan stilts, and Sienese arches all over the central part of the town, although antiquarian enthusiasms considerably reduce one's chances of survival in these congested streets. Two well-restored *case-torri* are those of the Accarigi in the short Costarella dei Barbieri leading up out of the Campo, and of the Piccolómini at the corner of Via Pantaneto and Via Follonica. These *duecento* towers and palaces are all of them stone-built.

The earliest of the large aristocratic palaces is that of the Tolomei, a huge block of masonry once without any openings on the unusually tall ground floor, except for the great doorways at the front and the back. Defence was of primary importance to the Tolomei, as well it might be in view of the fact that their first palace on this site, built in 1208, was destroyed sixty years later by their Ghibelline enemies. When the battle of Colle reversed political fortunes they returned to Siena and immediately started to rebuild, using materials from the palace of the arch-Ghibelline Provenzano Salvani which,

* On this point and on early buildings in general, see V. De Vecchi, *L'Architettura Gotica Civile Senese*, Siena, Accademia degli Intronati, 1950.

in accordance with the over-exuberant practice of the time, was demolished in its turn. As international bankers the Tolomei had contacts further afield than Pisa; the Guelf wind blew from Anjou; and their windows on the two upper floors were embellished with delicately fretted Gothic tracery in the French manner. The two doorways, however, were kept in the local style. That facing the piazza is particularly fine, with its Tolomei coats of arms and the projecting lions at the corner of the lintel. The lintel is straight and is placed a little below the springing of the pointed arch; the architect is feeling his way towards the true Sienese combination of arches, but has not quite got there. [*Plate* 5.]

Siena made great strides forward in the mid-thirteenth century. In 1245 we hear of an enlargement of the town's boundaries and the paving of the principal streets, the latter a step that Florence had taken a few years earlier. In another field, however, Siena outstripped her rival by over a century. *Lo Studio*, the university, was founded by scholars from Bologna in 1246. It was a civic foundation from the first, without an imperial charter. A decade later the learned Portuguese Pietro Hispano was teaching philosophy and medicine here. He then became Pope John XXI, whereas the scientific researches of his contemporary Capocchio da Siena aroused such consternation that he was burnt at the stake. This obvious failure to find a golden mean in the treatment of its men of learning may help to account for the sad fact that this university has never had any great distinction or influence. From the start its civic pay-masters seem to have gently discouraged any higher aim than the utilitarian one of providing the community with competent doctors and lawyers. The ancient university buildings, never very extensive or imposing, have gone, and virtually the only relic is the tomb of a medieval professor in the modern courtyard, with a relief which shows him addressing a class of students. Their desperate, goggling concentration arouses the envy of the modern lecturer.

With one great exception, one has to search for thirteenth-century architecture in Siena. The semi-circular Campo existed, but had no architectural pretensions; it lacked the Palazzo Pubblico and had shops, not palaces, round its upper side. Its shape is unique and has never been explained; can a theatre have stood here in Roman times? For want of a town hall, the council met in the church of San Cristoforo, but that was rebuilt in the eighteenth century except for its apse. Such of the smaller churches as are old have been smothered inside in bad Baroque, really bad Baroque, so that even Baroque-lovers wince a little on entering. One of them, San Giorgio in Pantaneto, was built immediately after Montaperti and named for the saint of the German allies who helped to win the battle. At least its old brick campanile with depressed arches is still there. Another memorial to that victory is the column in the Piazza Tolomei, though the she-wolf on top is later. Yet another is the great stone Antiporto di Camollía, built in preparation for the campaign. [*Plate* 1.]

A more interesting relic of Siena's first age is to be found in the public water supply. The oldest *fonte* is the famous Fontebranda, first mentioned in 1081, its present basin constructed in 1193, and vaulted over in 1246. The battlements are a recent but justified restoration in typically Sienese brickwork. Originally these battlements were more than a mere decorative addition, for at the earliest stage all the main *fonti* lay outside the city walls and were outposts whose defence was a matter of life and death. Despite the marble tablet on the east side and much jealous advocacy from Sienese men of letters, Dante's reference to Fontebranda in *Inferno*, 30, 76–78 is probably to a mountain spring of the same name in the Casentino. Beneath these time-worn arches the water stands green; it once flowed from one basin into the next; the first was for filling pitchers, the next for watering animals, the third for washing clothes, and there were two others lower still for bathing or industrial uses. Here Cecco used to meet his Becchina. The *fonte* is still used by washerwomen, though it is no longer a trysting-place for lovers, and modern reticence deters the inhabitants from taking their baths in so public a place. Instead, a small swimming-pool has replaced the lower tanks. [*Plate* 3.]

The Fonte Ovile on the other side of the town is nearly as old, as are the ruins of three others down in the outlying hollows. In 1295 the painter Duccio had a hand in siting the last of these big covered *fonti*, the Fonte Nuova; in that fortunate age civil engineering had not yet crossed the boundary that divides art from applied science.

Besides these half-dozen larger *fonti* there were some twenty-five smaller ones. They were fed by underground conduits or *bottini*, which by the end of the Middle Ages extended for over fifteen miles altogether. A formidable undertaking, but vulnerable in wartime; in the sieges of the sixteenth century some disused conduits had to be walled up lest the enemy should enter by them.

Sport can bind a community together nearly as much as walls and water-pipes. The medieval Sienese delighted in violent pastimes, such as knightly tournaments or the more popular *elmora*, a mock battle fought by teams of young men wearing light armour and carrying quarterstaves. Usually it was the Terzo di Città against the other two Terzi, the object being to drive the other side out of the Campo. In 1263 stone-throwing had to be forbidden, and after a final rousing match in 1291 in which 'ten gentlemen were slain, besides many of the baser sort', *elmora* was suppressed and *pugna*, fought with fists, was substituted. Played on one Continental sabbath in 1324, it developed into an unofficial *elmora* with improved armament such as axes and crossbows and, the magistrates having failed, it took the bishop and all his clergy to stop it. In its less lethal form this game was still popular in the sixteenth century. There were also the *asinate*, played between the smaller sub-divisions of the city, the *contrade* or wards, when thirty young men would try to get a donkey painted with their ward's colours first round the Campo against the obstruction of the other teams. These *asinate*, and the similar *buffalate* with buffaloes, were perhaps the genesis of the well-known *palio* race in its modern shape.

Palio means a banner, the trophy awarded for a race. How far these races go back in history is a vexed question. A Sienese *palio* is recorded as early as 1238, but it was a straightforward horse-race between single owners, held outside the northern gate. Later it was run inside the town, from the Porta Romana to the Duomo, on various religious festivals in the year, but the wards or *contrade* had nothing to do with it. Foreign potentates sometimes entered horses for it, and Cesare Borgia's jockey once had to be warned off the course. In the seventeenth century another kind of *palio* was started, a horse-race round the Campo with a large element of pageantry, rules allowing interference with other competitors, and no bloodstock. It was run between the *contrade*. From this race, itself almost certainly inspired by happy memories of the medieval *asinate* and *buffalate*, is descended the modern *palio* run on 2 July and 16 August. [*Plate* 8.]

Seventeen *contrade* have survived of an originally much larger number. How pale our 'neighbourhood unit', beloved of town-planning officers, seems in comparison! These *contrade*, on the slightest pretext, will send their standard-bearers forth into the streets, tow-wigged parti-coloured figures of fantasy, a cross between the knave of diamonds and those improbable young gallants frescoed on the walls of the Cathedral Library. As they begin to weave their vivid striped banners through the air, lambent against the dark background of a Sienese wall, they cease to be comic and become almost a work of art—at any rate a *comparsa* or 'fine appearance', which is the Sienese name for them. And the organizations are as flamboyant as their standard-bearers. Amply fortified with traditions, heraldry, honorific titles, office-holders, funds, and chapels, their rivalries a more excitable and much more complex version of those existing between Rangers and Celtic, ten of them enter horses for the race. The result is a great deal of spirited though well-managed pageantry followed by an all too brief period of total delirium as the competitors circle three times round the Campo. That night there is an open-air banquet in the street of the victorious *contrada*, presided over by the winning horse, appreciatively munching lumps of sugar at the head of the table. [*Plate* 9.]

In the modern *palio* Cesare Borgia's enterprising spirit has prevailed after all. How unimaginative, how defeatist, how very dull it would be for a *contrada* to trust solely, or even mainly, to the speed of its horse's legs. Anyway, the horses are drawn by lot and the jockeys, being strangers, can hardly be expected to appreciate how much it means to the *contrade* employing them that they should win, and to rival *contrade* that they should not. Both of these points of view must be put to them as cogently as possible, and suitable tactics worked out. With the officials and go-betweens of the ten competing *contrade* thinking and acting on these lines, the resulting manoeuvres both on and off the course and the recriminations immediately after the event would broaden the horizon of the most experienced steward of a Middle Eastern jockey club. Well, should one see the *palio*? Horse-lovers may be dissuaded; they will not approve of anything, least of all of the sharp downhill turn at the corner of the Campo. Art-lovers too, perhaps; at this season the city bursts its seams, the catering and traffic-control systems give up, the crowds are suffocating, and for a week on end it is out of the question to do anything except prepare to see the *palio*. Against this must be set the infectious excitement of the townsfolk, a splendid spectacle in a dramatic setting, the inspired massed flag-tossings, and the sheer fun of it.

In between these romps round the Campo, folk so vital and quick-witted could not fail to discover more subtle ways of letting off steam. The thirteenth-century Sienese began to take more than a casual interest in the arts. Before Duccio founded the Sienese school, painting hereabouts is often described by the vaguer and harsher adjective, 'Tuscan', although it is now held that its practitioners here were inspired less by Tuscan traditions than by others from farther south. The most interesting of several examples in the town and its neighbourhood is the *Madonna dagli Occhi Grossi* dating from round about 1230 and to be seen in the cathedral museum or Opera del Duomo. This is the altarpiece before which Buonaguida Lucari and his cornered fellow-citizens prayed before the battle. The painted wooden relief has an owlish, rustic appearance and is truly primitive, in the sense that it is without Byzantine or other obvious influences from some higher cultural source outside.

Soon after the middle of the century, however, the style changes and a distinctive Byzantine or nearly Byzantine manner appears. This is connected with the first painter's name known to us, that of Guido da Siena, the immediate forerunner of Duccio. But attributions to Guido are risky; this is still a field where the learned rage and the people imagine a vain thing. Most of the raging has centred round a small enthroned Madonna, or *Maestà*, signed by Guido da Siena with the date '1221' and now in the principal chamber of the Palazzo Pubblico. On stylistic grounds the date is several decades too early, and one of the many theories put forward was that some local artistic chauvinist—a breed rife in Italy from early times and not quite extinct today—had touched up the date, originally perhaps '1271', and so done his best to ensure that Guido da Siena should antedate the Florentine Cimabue. Modern techniques of examination, however, have shown that the date has not been altered, and Professor Carli has pronounced that '1221' is the date of an earlier Madonna which Guido completely repainted in the new style some fifty years later, retaining the original date to affirm the continued validity of a cult attached to the picture. To add to this complication, the faces have been repainted again about 1300, very probably by the great Duccio himself. [*Plate* 7.]

There are one or two other works by Guido's school in the Art Gallery, as well as an interesting *Virgin* in the Carmine church. And what may well be the oldest stained-glass window in Italy has been discovered since the war in the dilapidated church of the Madonna della Grotta some miles outside the town. It has been removed to the Gallery for restoration and safer keeping.

The large *Madonna del Bordone* in the church of the Servi, though of this period, is independent of Guido; it was painted by a Florentine prisoner of war, one Coppo di Marcovaldo, in the year after Montaperti, in order to ransom himself from his captors.

Other arts were keeping pace with painting. There is plenty of Romanesque sculpture to be found in churches in the district, though very little remains in the city itself. Most of these rural carvings, though attractive, are crude. More accomplished are the verses of Folcacchiero dei Folcacchieri, knight of Siena, who flourished about this time and again in Dante Gabriel Rossetti's translation. The knight was clearly something of a tactician:

Dolcie madonna, poi ch'eo mi moragio,
non troverai chi sí bene a te servire
tut'a tua voluntate.

Gentle my lady, after I am gone,
There will not come another, it may be,
To show thee love like mine.

The classic language of Tuscany has changed very little in seven centuries. Like the brickwork of the tower of San Giorgio, one cannot believe at first that it is so old.

The search for the thirteenth century in Siena, hitherto perhaps more diligent than rewarding, brings one at last to the cathedral. They started to build it in 1226 or possibly a year or two later. By 1260, when the people came in barefoot procession up the nave with heartfelt cries of '*Misericordia!*' and dedicated their threatened city to the Virgin, the essential features we see today were already there—the nave (without the clerestory), the crossing supporting the cupola, and the fine campanile. Within the next few years the church as originally planned was practically finished. This plan did not include the large choir which now extends to the east, nor did it envisage a western façade in anything like its present state of fantasy. [*Plates* 11, 12.]

As is usually the case with buildings of this period, the architect is unknown. From 1257 onwards we know that monks from San Galgano were in charge, but the contrast between this very Italian cathedral and the restrained French Gothic lines of their Cistercian abbey makes it as certain as anything can be that both the design and the original architect came from elsewhere.

The most obvious influence is that of Pisa, whose cathedral dates from considerably earlier. The Pisan architects, themselves inspired by a curious but attractive mixture of influences—Roman, Byzantine, Lombard, and Saracenic—developed some original decorative features of their own, of which the most pleasing is a profusion of small arcades and the most remarkable the use of different coloured marbles in bands. In the Duomo at Siena the former invention is scarcely represented, except for the spindly arcades round the cupola; the effect of the latter discovery is overwhelming and, to the Northern eye, unfortunate. Even the exuberant medieval Sienese found these zebra stripes too much for them and, in those parts of the building which were added later, placed the black layers much further apart. This subsequent restraint, as seen in the choir and the transepts, makes for more light and less bewilderment, though the visitor must decide for himself whether the overall result is better; once black stripes are used at all, to the detriment of restfulness and of any sense of upward movement, there is something to be said for using them wholesale to astound the spectator and suggest the city's heraldry.

These stripes are by no means the only eccentricity. All round the nave and the choir, above the great round arches, the projecting terracotta heads of the first hundred and seventy-two popes glare uncharitably down on the modern traveller from below an over-heavy cornice. One would have thought that a city which, though devout, was for long periods out of papal favour, might also have found them disturbing, even though it produced several of them in the course of history—nine, by the most generous reckoning. Perhaps the fewer, less obtrusive and less justified heads of the Roman emperors in the spandrels below were intended as some sort of Ghibelline counterweight. Actually all these heads date from the Renaissance.*

Odder still, the distances between the six piers which support the cupola are not equal. The irregularity can best be seen by glancing upwards at the unequal lengths of entablature above. Nor are the piers in the transepts placed quite symmetrically. The fact that the cupola does not cover the whole width of the nave and aisles is less remarkable, in view of the geometry of the arches and vaults. A similar arrangement is found at Piacenza. But it is hard to look at the structure of this church, one is so mesmerized by the black-and-white camouflage. The striped squinches in the rotunda, enclosing gilded statues, are undoubtedly the most bizarre feature of all.

In fact, the Duomo's internal architecture is more curious than beautiful, and it is for its embellishments that one revisits it. Most of these, such as the marvellous pavement, Duccio's rose-window, and the altars and marquetry and tombs, were added later, and will be described in the context of their own periods, as will the extensions to the building and the western façade.† Two poles fixed to piers of the crossing, popularly claimed to be those of the captured Florentine *carroccio*, call for an even greater effort of faith than do most ecclesiastical relics. They will scarcely detain the visitor on his way to see the greatest work of art that this first period produced.

Nicola Pisano's pulpit was commissioned in 1265 and finished in 1269, the year which saw the military disaster at Colle and the end of the Ghibelline epoch. It is an octagon resting on trefoil arches, themselves above slender pillars which stand alternately on the floor and on the backs of lions. On the flanks of the octagon are panels with scenes from the New Testament in relief, framed by figures in the round at the corners between them. The pulpit is certainly one of the finest things in Siena, both in its details and when seen as a whole. Stylistically it is a wonderful symbol of the moment it occupies in the city's history, standing as it does on the borderline between Romanesque and Gothic. Nicola Pisano came originally from the south of Italy, where the influence of Classical sculpture was exceptionally strong, so strong that some such expression as 'late Roman' gives a better idea of the prevailing style than does the word 'Romanesque'. The Roman sarcophagi which he must have seen in the Campo Santo at Pisa, where he worked before he came to Siena, doubtless strengthened this influence. As a result, he seems to jump from late Classical to Gothic without using the stepping-stone of Romanesque. In the Siena pulpit the Classical element is still strong, particularly in the seven reliefs, but Gothic has crept into most of the corner figures and has triumphed in the little arches supporting the octagon. Nicola's son Giovanni worked with his father on this pulpit, and it is reasonable to make him responsible for the greatest departures

* According to the malicious but seldom inaccurate Gibbon, the mythical Pope Joan had a place in the series. Certainly the head labelled Hadrian I is young and smooth and unlike all the others, and Hadrian lived in that colourful period of papal history in which Pope Joan was afterwards placed. Were the titles added or rewritten after the legend had been discredited?

† How the cathedral continued to grow is described at the ends of Chapters 4 and 6, and its Renaissance library is described at the end of Chapter 8.

from Classicism. The staircase was added in the late sixteenth century and does not offend.

This pulpit is one of a series by the Pisani, all superficially similar but all very different in detail and in style. It is interesting, when travelling through Tuscany, to compare it with the simpler and more Classical version that Nicola made nine years earlier for the baptistery at Pisa (having six instead of eight sides, bunched columns instead of statues at the corners, and less agitation among the figures in the reliefs), and with the pulpit Giovanni made some thirty years later for the church of Sant' Andrea in Pistoia (completely Gothic with its tall structure, pointed arches, and demented figures), and again with his still later one for the Duomo at Pisa, whose curved sides, broader horizontal courses, and almost Baroque-looking substitutes for arches show clearly that Giovanni at the end of his life was turning away from the Gothic. The pulpit at Siena, taken as an architectural whole, has a good claim to be regarded as the best of the four.

Despite a few great names, Siena never made sculpture an art of its own as it did painting. More than that, there is a strange gap between the two arts as practised here in this formative period. Siena's carving is derived from the Classical and its painting from the Byzantine. The two ways of seeing things are startlingly different. In the next two generations both arts were considerably modified by successive graftings with French Gothic, but in each case the original stock remained dominant and was never altogether bred out. One wonders what artists thought of this gap at the time when it was most pronounced. Did Guido da Siena and Nicola Pisano argue furiously about it?

Portal of west door, San Quirico d' Orcia

3

The Siena of the *Nove* as it was

HOW COULD EVEN romantics have believed that Siena started to decline soon after Montaperti? Yet the impression is not uncommon, and one widely read book in particular virtually closes its account of Sienese history at this point. This is like ending English history soon after Agincourt, with the failure of the Hundred Years' War. The Sienese of the time, who were too astute to be sentimentally Ghibelline for long, did not regard a reversal of foreign policy in that light. In fact the fall of the Hohenstaufen and the defeat at Colle cleared the space for a golden age.

In the years after 1269, then, the Sienese, caught between the upper and nether millstones of Florence and Charles of Anjou, abandoned a lost cause which had never quite agreed with their long-term aims. By some of the *grandi* this decision was accepted as imperative for the city-state's survival, but others of their order, perhaps a majority, clung to the past, and for a time the air in the narrow streets between the patrician fortress-towers was thick with counter-accusations and knife-blades. Those immediately below the *grandi*, on the other hand, were less attached to Ghibelline opinions, which they soon came to regard as an out-of-date aristocratic affectation bedevilling peace and trade. In 1277, therefore, these Whiggish merchants of the *popolo*, recognizing that Ghibelline sympathies were endemic in the class above them, carried through a bloodless revolution which removed the *grandi* from power. A few years later the council was reduced to Nine.

Throughout the rest of Sienese history, with brief exceptions, the great aristocratic families remained excluded from the highest political posts. They might wield considerable influence, but not direct personal power. Some such arrangement must obtain in any society which gravitates towards democracy while keeping a fairly rigid class structure. The Sienese did not devise a House of Lords, and their less ingenious solution could not have proved so permanent but for the lack of cohesion among the *grandi* themselves, who impetuously sacrificed their collective interest to their family feuds.

Doubtless the decisive factor which secured this quiet revolution was a shift in the economy from banking to wool, which took place about this time. The *grandi*, who were primarily international bankers, were harder hit than other citizens by four developments. In the first place the pope, misusing a spiritual sanction for political ends, had placed the unfilially Ghibelline city under an interdict, of which foreign debtors jumped to take advantage. Even after the interdict was lifted again, a good deal of custom remained permanently lost to other bankers. Secondly, Florence stole a march on other commercial towns by adopting the gold standard. The new golden florins, neatly stamped with the lily and John the Baptist, were soon recognized as a safer currency for international transactions than the debased silver coinage of other states, particularly after Florence had recovered from the war. Thirdly the leading Sienese bank, the *Magna Tavola* of the Buonsignori family, crashed for internal reasons at the end of the century. And lastly most of the remaining papal custom disappeared after the popes came under French control and left Rome for Avignon.

The wealth of the new ruling class was broader based. Prominent among its members were the wool merchants. Cloth was the staple manufacture of Siena as of most advanced medieval communities. Spinning and weaving were cottage industries, though the individual craftsmen in their homes were tied to a single merchant who supplied the wool and took most of the profit. The less skilled preliminary processes, such as carding, were carried out in small workshops under direct supervision. All these people lived and toiled in the deep hollow west of the town centre where springs of water could be found just within the walls. In this close-packed huddle of scourers, carders, spinners, weavers, fullers, and dyers, every activity was regulated by one of those dictatorial guilds usual in the Middle Ages, a vertical syndicate consecrated by over-frequent religious observances and dominated by the masters at the top. This woollen guild or *arte di lana* shared pre-eminence among the guilds, together with the two *arti* which ran foreign trade. But there was no formal distinction, as in Florence, between the greater and lesser guilds, nor did the Sienese guilds develop political ambitions in the same way as those in the larger city, where for a time they virtually took over the government.

Unfortunately the Sienese woollen trade was unable to expand beyond modest limits. The local wool crop was not of the best, and the water-supply within the walls was never quite enough. To the modern mind it seems odd that the industry was not moved out of the town to the banks of the Arbia or some other watercourse, but military and civic misgivings opposed any such move. Emotionally the city-state was as compact and walled-in as Ambrogio Lorenzetti's fresco of it. Instead of industrial dispersion, people set their hopes on tapping a mythical undergound river, the Diana, whose trickling was just perceptible to exceptionally loyal and sensitive ears on quiet nights—a form of optimism robustly derided by the chief spokesman of their commercial rivals:

Tu li vedrai tra quella gente vana
che spera in Talamone, e perderagli
più di speranza che a trovar la Diana;
ma più vi perderanno gli ammiragli.

> . . . Them shalt thou behold
> With that vain multitude, who set their hope
> On Talamone's haven; there to fail
> Confounded, more than when the fancied stream
> They sought, of Dian called; but they, who lead
> Their navies, more than ruined hopes shall mourn.*

The other reference in this uncharitable verse is to the bad luck which dogged Siena's attempts to find an outlet to the sea. Talamone, on the Maremma shore not far from Grosseto, was purchased in 1303, but to make a worth-while seaport of this malarial mudhole proved beyond the powers of medieval dredging and medicine. Even in the twentieth century it remains a dismal place.

In spite of this gradual slowing down of the economy, as compared with that of Florence, the age of the Nine was one of prodigious vigour, both public and private. Successful campaigns subdued the last feudal barons in the *contado*, in particular the Aldobrandeschi round Monte Amiata, and governors from the city took over the remaining feudal castles. The forfeited estates were mortgaged by the Nine to some of the great banking families, such as the Salimbeni; these presently became a new landed aristocracy, replacing the old, but more closely tied to the city. Siena doubtless derived more benefit from the change than did the peasants. Though wealth lagged behind the spectacular expansion further north, it was nevertheless very considerable, and fortunately for us an unusually large proportion of it was spent on the unique pictures and the splendid, severe buildings that we see today. The great Palazzo Pubblico with its tower, the Campo, the walls and gates, many of the family palaces, churches, and fountains—all this and more makes the early fourteenth century the supreme period of Sienese architecture as it was of painting.

In 1310, when the councillors moved into their newly-built Palace, a constitution came into force which vested all important power and patronage in the state in a self-perpetuating oligarchy. The Nine named their own successors in office, choosing exclusively Guelf merchants of the upper middle class, and thus creating a closed ruling caste, the *noveschi* or adherents of the *Nove*. Members of the council served for two months only, during which they lived in state and at public expense in the Palazzo Pubblico. The very short term of office interrupted a member's private business less and was a safeguard against corruption or tyranny, although it can hardly have made for efficient control of the details of administration. [*Plate* 22.]

In later ages governments of fat burghers have not had a good press. They are generally condemned as purse-proud, apprehensive, socially illiberal, and inglorious. In so far as these accusations fit the Nine, we can only be grateful for their conspicuous consumption of pigments, bricks and mortar, and admit that their fears of the anarchic *grandi* were well founded. Siena had its full share of Montague-and-Capulet blood feuds, romantic only at the distance of six centuries. There were frequent affrays between the

* *Purgatorio*, 13, 151–154 (Cary's translation).

Tolomei and the Salimbeni, the Piccolómini and the Malavolti, the Saracini and the Scotti. The worst trouble-makers, at least at first, were the Tolomei, whose pride asserted descent from the Ptolomies, and who went to the length of inciting the lower classes to riot with them. The fact that the dates of the bigger disturbances do not coincide with the four occasions when bad harvests caused hardship shows that this unrest was more personal than social. The Signory took effective counter-measures, keeping rigid control of the appointment of militia officers and introducing a permanent bodyguard of mercenaries under a *capitano di guerra* who, like the *podestà*, came from another city. They would have done better, of course, to extend political rights to the strata below their own. But urban democracy is not an easy growth, and even the Swiss towns at that time were strictly oligarchic.

The weakest side of the *Nove*, and indeed of all Sienese régimes, is shown in their dealings with the *contado*. Juridically and emotionally it was a conquered domain, subject to colonialism in its crudest sense. No attempt was made to extend some form of citizenship to its inhabitants, and little was done for their welfare. By means of price-control, export-banning, and tariffs, the rural economy was ruthlessly manipulated to provide cheap food for the city. Villagers paid direct taxes from which they derived very little benefit. In all this Siena was no worse than other city-states. But the long-term results were fateful, particularly in the military field. The countrymen, thus exploited, could not be recruited with profit or safety into the militia; the townsmen wished to be excused; the infantry arm was weakened and too much reliance was placed on small bodies of horse, often mercenaries; soon came the age of the *condottieri*, who blackmailed their employers and did their best to avoid occupational risks; and finally, in the sixteenth century, their showy armies collapsed before the businesslike pikemen of other countries.

For small powers an inglorious foreign policy usually makes sense. Siena belonged now to the Tuscan League, led by Florence. She purchased security and prosperity at the cost of sending contingents, which did not always distinguish themselves, to fight in Florentine wars against her old enemies in Arezzo or against those baleful and resounding tyrants, Uguccione della Faggiuola of Pisa and Castruccio Castracane of Lucca. In remaining loyal to this alliance, based on common interests and defence, the Nine can no more be accused of unworthy subservience to their country's former enemies than can Dr. Adenauer's government in more recent times. The test came when another emperor crossed the Alps. From 1310 to 1313 Henry of Luxemburg tried to restore the Empire in Italy. Of the Tuscan cities Pisa, followed by Arezzo, immediately declared in his favour, while Florence took the lead in opposing him. Siena, had she changed sides, might have tipped the balance, at least for a short time. But the Nine, sceptical of princes and deaf to Dante's trumpetings, kept their heads. Henry's coronation at Rome was enlivened by street warfare in which some Sienese troops took part, as they did in later operations near Florence. Henry paused hopefully before the gates of Siena, and then went on to take the waters for which the south-eastern part of the *contado* is famous, whereupon he died.

The Sienese, with an eye to their spa's reputation, encouraged rumours of poison deliberately administered by a fanatically Guelf priest, while the Florentine chronicler Villani, shaking his head over the misdeeds of this would-be conqueror of Italy, condemned most of all his grants to non Florentines of the right to coin florins. Villani's town is, among other things, the Aberdeen of Italy.

Is it possible that the rulers of Siena, Guelf but not papalist, played some part in defeating the extravagant pretensions of Boniface VIII? William of Nogaret, sent by Philip the Fair to effect the pope's overthrow, established himself in the castle of Staggia, just inside the Sienese border, in order to conduct his nefarious negotiations for the coup d'état at Anagni. It is difficult to believe that the Nine, who had their intelligence service, knew nothing of this, and the cardinal of Siena was certainly in the plot.

The Nine also had a better documented success in 1343, when they helped the Florentines to get rid of their unpopular despot the duke of Athens, who had offended Siena as well. Even so hostile a witness as Villani admits that the three hundred Sienese horse and four hundred crossbowmen whom he saw entering his town to settle accounts with the duke were '*molto bella gente*'; and in fact they played the leading part as intermediaries in securing the tyrant's capitulation and escorting him and his household out of town. During the interregnum it appears that the white-and-black flag of Siena flew alone for three days over the Florentine Palazzo Vecchio.

At home, to judge from the spirited verse of contemporary Sienese poets, life seems to have been one long carnival, celebrated elegantly in Folgore's circle and earthily in Cecco's. Folgore's sonnets describing the amusements of Siena's *jeunesse dorée* do not survive Victorian translations:

> Comes Blithesomeness with mirth and merriment,
> All decked in flowers she seemeth a rose-tree;
> Of linen, silk, cloth, fur, now beareth she
> To the new knight a rich habiliment . . .

and the translator, J. A. Symonds, himself unkindly remarks that, to Northerners, Folgore's ideal knight 'would have seemed but little better than a scented civet-cat'. Knighthood, though still conferred by city councils and more expensively by visiting emperors, was already becoming an anomaly in the Italian communes.

Folgore wrote to immortalize the 'spendthrift brigade'; Dante transferred their follies to a whole people:

> *Ed io dissi al poeta: 'Or fu giammai*
> *gente sí vana come la sanese?*
> *certo non la francesca sí d'assai.'*
>
> Then to the bard I spake: 'Was ever race
> Light as Siena's? Sure not France herself
> Can show a tribe so frivolous and vain.'*

At times there is a positively German quality about Dante.

* *Inferno*, 29, 121–123 (Cary's translation).

While Folgore's sometimes over-delicate verse is a late echo of the troubadours, Cecco's poems are realistic and often malicious, an anticipation of Villon. Cecco had a difficult life. Apart from the grave disapproval of Dante's circle, he had to contend with a twittery mother and a highly conventional banker father. Messer Angiolieri's plan for his bohemian son's '*ristorazion*' was to marry him to an outstandingly silly woman of his own class, 'who chattered like a thousand guitars', but Cecco burst out of the old family house in the narrow street to pursue his socially unsuitable mistress and the career of an angry young man.

If I were fire, I'd burn the world away;
If I were wind, I'd turn my storms thereon;
If I were water, I'd soon let it drown;
If I were God, I'd sink it from the day;
If I were Pope, I'd never feel quite gay
Until there was no peace beneath the sun;
If I were Emperor, what would I have done?——
I'd lop men's heads all round in my own way.
If I were Death, I'd look my father up;
If I were Life, I'd run away from him,
And treat my mother to like calls and runs.
If I were Cecco (and that's all my hope),
I'd pick the nicest girls to suit my whim,
And other folk should get the ugly ones.*

Becchina, the cobbler's daughter, had a personality which at any rate helped to save him from the tiresome theme of courtly love. There is life, not artificial romance, in Becchina as seen by Cecco, ranging from

When I behold Becchina in a rage,
Just like a little lad I trembling stand;*

to

Becchina wants so much of all that's nice
Not Mahomet himself could yield enough;*

or

I am enamoured, and yet not so much
But that I'd do without it easily;
And my own mind thinks all the more of me
That Love has not quite penned me in his hutch.
Enough if for his sake I dance and touch
The lute, and serve his servants cheerfully:
An overdose is worse than none would be.*

* Dante Gabriel Rossetti's translations, in his *Early Italian Poets* (Routledge, 1905).

A few renounced the art, the politics, and the gaieties of Siena's greatest age. In 1313 the learned Giovanni Tolomei, rather than take part any more in the life of the university or the feuds and ambitions of his family, went out with two other nobles—a Piccolomini and a Patrizi—and founded a hermitage in the forlorn *creta* country to the south. He took the name of Brother Bernardo. They and those who joined them slowly reclaimed the dry soil, planting olive trees on a ridge among the wrinkled landslips. Thus arose the great monastery of Monte Oliveto and a new religious order, small but distinguished; one that remained truer to its founder's ideals than some others. Nor was it an ivory tower. When the pestilence struck Tuscany, Brother Bernardo and his monks, thirty-five years older, left their flourishing monastery and went to help their own and other cities. Many of them, including the founder, gave their lives in this way. It is ironical that St. Catherine is so much better known.

The golden age passed, doubtless without being fully appreciated until afterwards. The middle 1340s were bad years. Werner von Uerslingen, 'the enemy of God, of pity and of mercy', ravaged the *contado*, the first of many wandering soldiers of fortune to do so. There was an economic depression that started in Florence. The pope, short of money, demanded payment of old debts due from the Buonsignori bank and, on being refused, put Siena under another interdict. In the spring of 1348 the Black Death spread swiftly through the country from Genoa, whose shipping had brought it from the Levant. The city's population, probably approaching 50,000, was cut to little more than a third, and the loss was never fully made good until our own time. As to what it felt like then, we have the stark description of a Sienese chronicler:

> 'Men and women died almost without warning. A lump came in the groin or in the armpit, and while they spoke of it they fell dead. . . . No one accompanied them to the graveyard, neither relatives nor friends nor clergy, nor were the last rites performed. And I, Agnolo di Tura called the stout, buried five of my children in one trench with my own hands, and many others did likewise. And some were so badly buried that the dogs dug them up and ate them, dragging their bones through the city. And no bells tolled, and no one mourned, however great his loss, for almost everyone expected his own death. And as the plague went on folk thought that no one would remain alive, and men believed and said: This is the end of the world.'

4

The Siena of the *Nove* as it is

THE AGE OF the Nine created the Siena we know. More than half of the things one sees and remembers here are the memorial of that sober merchant polity. Duccio, Simone Martini and the flowering of the Sienese school, the Palazzo Pubblico and the Gothic domestic architecture derived from it, Giovanni Pisano's façade for the cathedral, the town-planning, walls and gates—these are among the period's achievements, and the attempt to enlarge the Duomo its only great failure.

One must take a little trouble to appreciate Sienese painting. The first step is the hardest. To most of us, medieval religious symbolism means very little, and the average British visitor to the city's Art Gallery, after working conscientiously through several rooms containing virtually nothing else, finds the knowledge that the Gallery has a second floor beginning to weigh on him. From the books on Italian art that he has recently re-read he recalls that the Sienese school is described as a wayward offshoot from the main stream, or even more unkindly as a backwater. Why go any further up it?

The answer is that with a little time, effort, and knowledge these almond-eyed saints and Virgins begin to exercise a quite extraordinary fascination. This post-Byzantine formula for transmuting the human face and figure so as to suggest the numinous is a most powerful and expressive language of the spirit. The formula has a hundred subtle variations, and few experiences are more exciting than to begin to find one's way among them. One need not share the artists' theology to be moved by this painting, any more than one need become a Hindu to appreciate Indian art. But one must become accustomed to the language. Then one wonders whether any other idiom can compete with it in its own field. What later sacred art, at least, has avoided so well the traps of sentiment, grandiloquence, or absurdity?

Our visitor's other common fault is to attempt to explore the whole sequence of Sienese painting at once. Instead, he should be ruthlessly selective. He should concentrate exclusively on the great period, on Duccio and his successors up to 1350, and only after he has come to understand and like these pictures should he venture among the prickly polyptychs, queer visions, moonstruck ecstasies, and frothy confections that come later.

Sienese painting of the earlier *trecento*, then, though its subject-matter is restricted, is one of the great achievements of European art, and the effort spent in getting to know it will repay one for a lifetime. But first the essential minimum of background knowledge must be there.

Duccio di Buoninsegna was Dante's contemporary. Each of them achieved greatness by accepting a conservative artistic tradition and enlarging its possibilities. They were both masters of symmetry. Both used highly organized art-forms with meticulous care to express a mystical intuition of superhuman dignity and beauty. The work of both has lasted six centuries and more. And both great men were their own enemies in their dealings with others. Both had the unreasonable, quixotic, improvident temperament called 'artistic'. Both were romantic reactionaries who failed to come to terms with the political evolution of their day. Duccio's recusancy did not lead him as far as exile, a fate to which writers are necessarily more prone than painters, but perhaps it brought him the heavy fine he had to pay as a young man; and at the turn of the century, when all sensible people had long since settled down under the new Guelf dispensation, we find him refusing to swear allegiance to the *capitano del popolo* and his Whiggish ordinances or to take the field with the militia against Ghibelline barons in the *contado*. For these offences he incurred three more fines, while his thriftlessness resulted in several judgements for debt. He even seems to have got into trouble for having dealings with witchcraft.

In our own age, with a comparable record, he might well have found himself passed over when it came to further public commissions, but the Sienese ethos was less primly bureaucratic than ours, and anyway no one else could paint like he could. Yet the authorities, if enlightened, were not imprudent. In 1308, when they engaged him to paint a new central altarpiece for the cathedral, their experience led them to insist on his signing a contract which, with its time-limits, specifications, and penalty-clauses, was almost as great a masterpiece in its own way as the universally acclaimed *Maestà* which, his energies thus canalized, he finished within the agreed three years. [*Plate* 18.]

Its impact on his fellow-citizens was tremendous. On a June day in 1311 the bells were rung, a public holiday was declared, and a huge procession, in which the Nine, the bishop, and everyone else took part with lighted candles in their hands, carried the great picture from Duccio's house in Via Stalloreggi by way of the Campo up to the cathedral. The pleasant mingling of religious and patriotic emotions on that day is described in some detail by the chronicler, but conveyed to us more directly by the naïve pride of the words that Duccio himself placed at the bottom of his panel, praying the Virgin to grant peace to his city and life to himself because he had painted her thus:

Mater sancta Dei—Sis causa Senis requiei,
Sis Ducio vita—Te quia pinxit ita.

Two years after this triumph, for which he was generously rewarded in terms of money, he went bankrupt. His large family was left with nothing on his death, though some of his sons carried on his *bottega*.

What was Duccio aiming at as a painter? Unlike his slightly younger contemporary Giotto, he did not repudiate the Byzantine artistic ideal. He was more interested in the possibilities of a flat design of shapes and colours, defined and brought to life by a rhythmic line, than in any attempt to render natural appearances more convincingly. He bequeathed this choice to the whole Sienese school, which consequently branched off from the rest of Italian painting. The latter, with Florence in the lead, became increasingly 'solid' and naturalistic, whereas the Sienese, though presently wandering a long way from Duccio, continued in the main to depict various dream worlds of their own. Not that Duccio was unable to render spatial depth if he wanted to; to see this one has only to look at those of the small scenes from the back of the *Maestà* which have an architectural setting, and at their ceilings in particular. But his figures, apart from their faces, are curiously static; they lack tangibility, and the efforts they make are inward, not physical. Their minds are under the severest strain, but not one of them really supports or lifts a weight. This rejection of the physical, which was for the most part deliberate, is by no means a fault in a painter of religious subjects. Modern art has cured us of insisting on naturalism in a picture, or even of wanting very much of it, so that the visitor nowadays is in a much better position to appreciate Duccio than was his counterpart a generation or two ago. Today these majestic, sad, unearthly Byzantine forms seem a less inappropriate symbol for the Divine than the all too anthropomorphic productions of other Italian schools.

The air around Duccio and his immediate followers has long been thick with the assured but conflicting pronouncements of art-historians and the hum of their apparatus. Attributions, dates, influences, and evolutions of style are still disputed. The most recent and magisterial studies of a thorny subject are those of Professor Carli, himself a Sienese and the artistic curator for the city and province. The reader should consult his works, some of which have been published in English versions.

It is now generally agreed that Duccio, and not the Florentine master Cimabue as was thought for centuries, was wholly or mainly the creator of the *Rucellai Madonna*, which he painted in Florence in 1285 before he was thirty, and where it still is. The exact degree of influence which Cimabue exercised over him at that time is more doubtful, but at least he seems to have been a member of this Florentine circle for a year or two. Shortly before that he painted two other supremely beautiful things, the *Madonna di Badia a Isola*, still out there in the country, and the *Madonna di Crevole*, now in the Opera del Duomo at Siena. In 1288 he designed the rose-window in the cathedral choir, the earliest Italian stained-glass window on such a scale. After that came the graceful *Madonna of the Franciscans*, the *Maestà*, and the last work that can be attributed to him with certainty, the large *Polyptych No. 47* in the Art Gallery. [*Plates* 51, 13.]

In this sequence of paintings there is a clear progress away from stiffness and towards a more masterly elegance of line. The hems and folds of robes show this as well as anything. The Byzantine is beginning to thaw into Gothic. But do Duccio's later pictures gain from this greater elegance as much as they lose in their crisp stylization and in their power to inspire awe? To the writer at least the *Madonna di Crevole*, with its plain gold background, its unrelieved Byzantine severity, and the extraordinary rigid grace of the dark gold-webbed figure, is the most moving picture he painted.

The series of intense glimpses of the Gospel story formerly on the back of the *Maestà* have been described and analysed superbly by Berenson. He gives high praise to their expressiveness and their composition, but finds that they do not communicate the sensations of life. Perhaps they were not altogether meant to. Was not Duccio trying to penetrate to some archetypal truth beyond these scenes, to illustrate destiny as well as incident? Does not his art rise to its greatest height when he is least 'tactile' and closest to the Byzantine tradition, as in the three Maries at the tomb?

Some time ago these scenes, for the sake of more convenient display, were detached from the back of the *Maestà* by the simple expedient of sawing the thick panel into two thinner ones. During this lighthearted undertaking the saw went through the Madonna's face on the front, and after it the tendency of the wood to warp was doubled. The great front panel has been restored in 1960 by the Institute at Rome. It has been cleaned and preserved but not, of course, repainted, except for minute areas done with vertical brush-strokes to distinguish them from the original. Everything else is the authentic work of Duccio.

Among Duccio's closest followers were Segna di Bonaventura (who was probably his nephew), Ugolino di Nerio (whose *Madonna Addolorata*, No. 596 in the Gallery, is one of the most moving of all Sienese pictures) and the Master of Città di Castello—not to mention Ugolino Lorenzetti, who never existed at all, at least with that name, but who was invented by Berenson to account for certain pictures which combine the styles of Ugolino di Nerio and Pietro Lorenzetti. Moreover, Professor Carli thinks he is identical with the anonymous master whose curious transitional *Madonna* hangs in the church of San Pietro Ovile, and some of whose other works are in the Art Gallery. It is, in fact, a formidably complicated subject.

To these earnest disciples Simone Martini must have seemed rather a tiresome young man. His contacts were much wider than theirs. He brought in a further substantial measure of international Gothic to blend with Duccio's later style. He took big steps forward in the use of perspective. He was often absent from Siena for long periods and finally went off to the papal court at Avignon. Only four years after Duccio had finished his *Maestà*, Simone Martini was commissioned by the Nine to paint another one on the wall of their larger council-chamber, presumably because Duccio did not paint frescoes. With this magnificent picture of 1315, his earliest known work, Simone Martini did much to close that curious gap between the arts and to cure that double vision from which artists in Siena had been suffering.* That is to say, he brought his painted figures into focus with Giovanni Pisano's statues, or very nearly so. Only their eyes are still Sienese. The Virgin of this new *Maestà* has been de-Byzantinized, her robes flow freely in the Gothic manner, her throne and its canopy have Gothic ornaments and are given reality by improved perspective, while the attendant saints are neatly marshalled in

* See the last paragraph of Chapter 2 (p. 38).

depth. Compared with Duccio's panel this picture, though time has treated it worse, is far more lifelike and graceful. But it is not nearly so numinous. Simone Martini has brought his heavenly court a long way down towards the earth; in fact to the modern eye some of them look as if they were posing happily for a group photograph. [*Plate* 19.]

The artist himself may possibly have come to feel something of the sort, for the panel pictures he painted four or five years later at Pisa and at Orvieto are decidedly more 'Sienese' and traditional in every way. To the writer's far from expert eye, at least, Simone Martini's style appears to fluctuate more than would be accounted for by the change of media or than some of the authorities admit. In his Assisi frescoes the manner and feeling are again quite different, and yet another change marks his final period at Avignon. Duccio develops fairly steadily in one direction, whereas Simone is a restless painter, never satisfied for long with his own innovations. Obviously the most consistent feature in his work is his line, of which he had unerring mastery; it flicks through the air like an angler's cast. Using it in his most delicate and 'Sienese' style, he achieved his masterpiece, the *Annunciation* in the Uffizi which everyone knows.

Even when commemorating a soldier he does not aim primarily at naturalism. The symbolic, dreamlike essence of Sienese art is still very much there. At the other end of the council-chamber, opposite the *Maestà*, the matter-of-fact *Guidoriccio* does not ride through the semi-abstract landscape he has conquered, but is super-imposed upon it—a brilliant conception, wonderfully executed—while the siege is depicted without any busy little human figures, but merely, and much more tellingly, by the investing palisades with spears and Sienese shields and the commanders' heraldry displayed round their tents. This was the memorial that the grateful Nine voted to their *capitano di guerra* after he had recaptured the rebellious castle of Montemassi in the hills towards Grosseto. Members of later governments, whose relations with their generals were less harmonious, must often have looked a little wryly at this vast military figure dominating their deliberations.* [*Plate* 16.]

When Simone Martini does use human figures to tell a story, his illustrations are vivid and touched with a childlike surprise. The miracles of the Blessed Agostino Novello in the church of Sant' Agostino, and the balcony accident in particular, are *trecento* Stanley Spencers, just a little larger than life, with the observed fantasy of everyday things suddenly transformed into the miraculous. [*Plate* 15.]

The Gallery has recently acquired another of his works. In 1957 a friend of the writer's, Don Riccardo Sprugnoli, then the parish priest of Lucignano d'Arbia, brought in for repair the artless Baroque Madonna from his village church. Close examination showed that the fine network of cracks that covered it belonged less to the surface of about 1600 than to a buried stratum of painting. This implied a considerably earlier painting underneath. Was it worth 'excavating', a process that involves the destruction of whatever is on top? The parishioners would have something to say if their Madonna were obliter-

* Villani mentions a *battifolle* or temporary fort used by the Sienese in this siege to protect their catapult against sudden sorties. The enemy sent them a rude note demanding its removal. Presumably this is the curious castellated affair depicted in the centre background.

ated to no purpose. Don Riccardo, a strong character, was prepared to accept the risk. Millimetre by millimetre, an eye of the lower level was uncovered, a clear sad almond-shaped eye, an eye, as Professor Carli at once declared with awe-struck certainty, that only Simone Martini could have painted. [*Plate* 20.]

The kerchief and robe are missing, except for small blue fragments, and in accordance with the austere canons of today no attempt has been made to restore them. It seems probable that some inferior pigment was used for this part of the picture; it deteriorated with time and made the Madonna so unsightly that some undistinguished artist of 1600 was given the task of repainting her, an operation which, once begun, was done overall after the heavy fashion of the day. In spite of this, the essentials are in excellent condition and constitute a picture of great beauty, clearly belonging to the same 'traditional' phase as Simone's two *Virgins* at Orvieto. The Child is new-born and rigidly swaddled, and the Mother's pose is, most unusually for the period, a rightward one. How many more *trecento* pictures lie unsuspected beneath the cracking paintwork of bucolic altarpieces, the victims of post-Renaissance contempt for the 'primitive'? [*Plate* 21.]

The villagers of Lucignano had long been used to a bovine Madonna, and not even Don Riccardo's considerable gifts of eloquence could persuade them to venerate a feline one. In view of their mutinous and unenlightened attitude, the picture was transferred to the Siena Gallery, where it has filled a notable gap in the collection.

Simone Martini's brother-in-law, Lippo Memmi, was not a painter of the first rank. His part in the Uffizi *Annunciation* is now considered minimal. His best work at Siena is a *Virgin* in the church of the Servi. The colours are wonderfully fresh, though the picture lacks the religious depth of Segna's more traditional one next to it. But only a little less eminent than Duccio and Simone are the last two Sienese painters of the period, the brothers Lorenzetti.

Pietro Lorenzetti, the elder of the two, was the first Sienese expressionist. He is at his most characteristic in the Passion frescoes at Assisi, which many find altogether too dramatic. A striking *Crucifixion* on a red ground, in San Francesco at Siena, shows something of this quality. The strength and simplicity of the design are as impressive as the figures are theatrical. Much the same applies to a *Massacre of the Innocents* in the Servi. An earlier work of his, more solid and less emotional, is the *Birth of the Virgin* in the Opera del Duomo, a triptych with two of its three scenes run together. It enables us to look inside a Sienese *trecento* palace. No. 84 in the Art Gallery is also interesting; it shows the early Carmelites in the wilderness wearing their peculiar horizontally banded habits; and the figures moving in a landscape (which is obviously the *creta* country near Siena) are an innovation in Sienese art.

Ambrogio Lorenzetti is more meditative. He is best known for his frescoes of *Good and Bad Government*, of which more in a moment. Of his panel-paintings one in particular stands out, the figure of St. Dorothy in triptych No. 77. Though St. Dorothy is rapt in mystical contemplation, there is nothing wishy-washy about the picture; she is as strong as an oak. But the rest of the triptych is unsuccessful. Ambrogio's two little landscapes (Nos. 70 and 71) make one wish he had done more of them. Incidentally, the little town by the sea is almost certainly the Talamone from which so much was hoped at the time. And No. 65, a small *Madonna*, marks another milestone in the rendering of depth, to which end the carpet as well as the placing and the relative clarity of the figures all contribute; the last angels almost blend into the arched gold behind the Virgin's head. When forced by his patrons to depict drama rather than contemplation, he does it in a curiously static way, as in his pair of frescoes in the Franciscan church, where even the martyrdom of the missionary friars at Ceuta is being done statically and, to slow things down still more, he has peopled this place opposite Gibraltar with impassive Chinese.*

The companion fresco succeeded better, and the intrigues that brought down the over-mighty Boniface VIII come to life again as we see him surrounded by these shifty-looking cardinals, while shallow over-dressed young men from Folgore's and Cecco's circle look on. [*Plate* 23.]

Another of Ambrogio's more remarkable pictures is the *Madonna del Latte* in the seminary next San Francesco; she is slit-eyed and fiercely maternal like a mother-ferret as she watches the delighted gulpings at her breast. [*Plate* 26.]

How did painting come to play so large a part in Sienese life? In spite of its decorative, ultra-elegant quality it was not a court art, nor was it aristocratic. Instead, many layers of society contributed their lively interest and their money to make it possible—the government, rich merchant families, orders, congregations, guilds. Carli ascribes the phenomenon to the interaction of pride and piety, both exceptionally strong in this emotional city. But other Italian towns were proud and pious, without giving birth to so sustained and distinctive an output of pictures, and a British observer might attach equal importance to the effect of habit. The Sienese community, unlike ours at any period, got used to the idea that it could not live without new pictures. For the sensitive, they became an essential enhancement of their emotional life, and for the practical, an accepted symbol of vitality and success. For all, they were a national heritage to be added to. The tradition, once established in the relatively peaceful and prosperous time of the *Nove* through the excitement generated by a group of artists of genius, outlasted the peace and prosperity—and, it must be admitted, to some extent the genius.

Being a public art, some of its principal works glorify the rooms in the Palazzo Pubblico from which the Nine and subsequent councils ruled the city. These frescoes are at least as interesting as historical documents as they are impressive aesthetically. Below Simone Martini's *Maestà*, for instance, is a rhyming inscription, novel in its social content as well as in its choice of Italian instead of Latin, which makes it clear that, if the strong exploit the weak, any prayers offered on behalf of the former will be unavailing:

Ma se i potenti a' debil fien molesti,
Gravando loro con vergogna e danni,
Le vostre orazion non son per questi.

* Or, more accurately speaking, with Mongols in their national dress. How did Ambrogio come to see them? Did he perhaps meet the diplomatic mission which one of Kublai Khan's successors sent to the papal court in 1338? These pictures point down so many fascinating historical bypaths.

It must surely have shaken the self-assured merchant oligarchy when Simone Martini had to repaint this fresco only six years after he had finished it. The excise department had stored salt in the next room, and their notorious oppression of the weak, then as in all ages, coupled with saline damp in the wall, had caused the Virgin and her smiling court to vanish.

In the *Nove*'s smaller council-chamber are Ambrogio Lorenzetti's frescoes of *Good and Bad Government*, dating from 1337 to 1343. They have been much damaged by time, but the main features of Good Government are clear enough when the light is good, although unfortunately the artist was not content with depicting the mundane blessings that flowed from his patrons' enlightened rule—the trade, building, and dancing within the city's gates, and the husbandry and hunting outside them. The details of this part of the fresco are a delightful if idealized social commentary, from the bridal cavalcade on the extreme left to the trading port of Talamone on the right, and repay close examination. The rest of this large fresco is a mistaken attempt to base a pictorial allegory on the *Politics* of Aristotle, a work then much in vogue. Those on whom this intolerably long-winded treatise has been inflicted in youth may be able to identify the figures of the various virtues which the philosopher deemed specially applicable to Good Government —Prudence, Fortitude, Temperance, Distributive Justice, and the like—and will note the three Christian virtues hovering uncertainly overhead on a smaller scale. Or else one can peer at the labels with which the artist has equipped these abstractions, perhaps at the request of some obtuse councillor who disliked all this classical tomfoolery. As a small boy, when I was first shown all this, I was convinced that the clearest and best-known figure of all, that of Peace reclining distended in an uneasy posture, had strayed from the fresco of Bad Government and symbolized Indigestion. [*Plates* 24 and 25, 17.]

Ambrogio reminds us that Siena, like everywhere else in the Middle Ages, was an uncomfortable place for non-conformists and the maladjusted. This scholastic concept of Good Government includes several instances of capital punishment and a heavily guarded drove of luckless prisoners, due to be herded down the aptly named Via dei Malcontenti at the back of the Palazzo.

A detail in this picture explains the rows of cavities pitting the Palazzo's façade. The architect left these holes not out of kindness to the pigeons but to hold scaffolding-beams horizontally, thus doing away with the need for upright supports. The masons at work on Ambrogio's skyline are standing on scaffolding of this sort. [*Plate* 24.]

There are several other small rooms on this floor, one of them alive and wriggling with frescoes by Spinello Aretino. These depict incidents in the struggle which took place over two hundred years earlier between the Emperor and Pope Alexander III, who was born in Siena. No one would have been more surprised at this tribute to Alexander III than the Sienese consuls of his time who, though they had their differences with Barbarossa, quarrelled with Alexander so violently that they recognized the anti-pope who is being triumphantly burnt at the stake in the final scene. These frescoes too are good documentary; a medieval sea-fight must have been just like that.

The primacy of painting in Siena has made us approach the Palazzo Pubblico by way of the pictures inside it, but this unusual procedure implies no slight, for architecturally it ranks among the great town halls of Europe. True, it has only one magnificent façade, but this is a superb creation, enhanced by the blending of stone with brick and still more by the slightly forward angle of the wings. Seen across the ribs in the pavement of the scallop-shaped Campo, which curve three-dimensionally, it is as effective to the eye as it is baffling to the amateur camera. [*Frontispiece*, *Plates* 1 and 29.]

Until it was built, the council had usually met in the church of San Cristoforo, while its officers had managed as best they could in various makeshift buildings. The great palace was begun in 1298 and finished in 1310. It was then the same as we see it now, except that the wings were a storey lower, as is evident from the corbel-table marking the original level of the roof. These ornamental corbel-tables, with triangular corbels below the little rounded blind arcades, are a feature of Sienese architecture, as are the equally Sienese arches on the ground floor, whose origin was described in Chapter 2. The top storeys were added to the wings in the late seventeenth century and harmonize surprisingly well. The heraldic decorations, besides the white-and-black shield of the commune and the lion of the *popolo*, include the arms of the sixteenth-century Medici Grand Dukes and, high up, the emblem of San Bernardino's religious revival, which was also added later.

The tower, 334 feet high, is disproportionately large when seen from the front, much better from the lower far corner of the Campo, and so splendid a thing that one at once forgives it its undue size. Started in 1325, with two brothers Rinaldi from Perugia as architects, it was completed by Agostino di Giovanni in 1344 except for some minor details. The painter Lippo Memmi designed the lily of stonework which bursts out of the tall brick shaft with all its machicolations, battlements, and bell-housings. Its name, Torre di Mangia, comes from the manikin who strikes the hours and who replaced the original bell-ringer, a cheerfully improvident character nicknamed *Mangiaguadagni* or 'spendthrift'.

At the foot of the tower stands a curious open chapel which was begun as a thank-offering by those who escaped the Black Death. Its mixture of styles shows that, rather disgracefully, it took a long time to finish. Much of it dates from the 1370s, while the Renaissance frieze was added by Federighi nearly a century later.

At the far corner, as Evelyn the diarist noted when he came here in 1644, are 'the statues of Romulus and Remus with the Wolf, all of brasse, plac'd on a columne of ophite stone. . . . These ensignes being the armes of the towne, are set up in divers of the streetes and publiq wayes both within and far without the citty.' [*Plate* 29.]

The Palazzo Pubblico consolidated a local style in domestic architecture, just as Duccio's virtually simultaneous *Maestà* may be said to have inaugurated the Sienese school of painting. From now on palaces were built partly or mainly of brickwork. Already the Nine had decreed that all new buildings round the Campo must have Gothic windows divided by small columns. Subsequent rebuilding has robbed this piece of town-planning of its full effect, but the vast Palazzo Sansedoni remains to show us what an impressive motonony it aimed at, a monotony augmented in this case by an eighteenth-century restoration. Almost all the leading families followed suit, whether their property faced the Campo or not. The Palazzo Salimbeni, now the Monte dei Paschi bank, is the largest of all, but is spoilt aesthetically, though not from the medieval faction-leader's or the modern banker's standpoint, by the formidable blank wall below. And it has been over-restored. Better examples of the *Nove* style are the right-hand wing of the Hospital, the Palace of the Captain of War, where Guidoriccio's successors lived, and the Palazzo Chigi-Saracini, built for the Marescotti whose eagle arms adorn every window. The tower of this last is, if not the original, at least the successor of that from which the town drummer watched the battle of Montaperti away to the east and shouted down his commentary to the anxious non-combatants below. [*Plates* 9, 28.]

The Palazzo Buonsignori (now the Art Gallery) might well be mistaken for a slightly over-restored building of the *trecento*. In fact it is a telling tribute to the conservativism of the mid-fifteenth century. There are also many examples of smaller *trecento* houses. One, with more elaborately decorative brickwork than most, is half-way down the Via dei Rossi on the right. Another, between the Palazzo Buonsignori and the neighbouring church, is popularly known as the house of La Pia, after a dame who was murdered in far-away wastes by her faithless husband;

> '*Siena mi fe'*, *disfecemi Maremma,*'
> 'Siena made me, Maremma unmade me,'

she wailed to Dante. It seems, however, that it was a harsh theological doctrine and not his customary xenophobia that made him put this unfortunate and apparently blameless Sienese lady in ante-purgatory.*

These brick Gothic palaces are attractive and practical. The fact that this style was pounced on by the Victorians and transplanted to murky Midland towns with unfortunate results, should not blind us to its great merits when first devised.

Another legacy of the period is the outer circuit of ramparts, the ones that, despite some building that is now taking place beyond them, are still very much in evidence to anyone entering the city. The old brick wall plunges down heughs and up again with a Chinese scorn for gradients, embracing the outlying *fonti*, or most of them, as well as the jumble of close-packed building on the summits. The finest gate is the Porta Romana, a great embattled structure of brick enclosing a forecourt and decorated with a fresco, often re-painted and now gone except for a few of Sassetta's angels—he caught pneumonia while painting them. The Píspini and Ovile gates are nearly as fine, and above the narrow Porta Camollía is a pleasant inscription of the early Baroque period, *Cor magis tibi Sena pandit,* Siena opens her heart to you wider than this. [*Plate* 45.]

There were never enough *fonti*, and the meagre water-supply on this densely-populated hilltop was a most serious problem for the Nine. Their search for more water within the city boundaries ended in Dante's sarcasms and a very deep but unproductive well in what is now the Carmine convent. Nothing daunted, at great cost and trouble

* *Purgatorio*, 5, 133–136.

they built a conduit from springs near Querciagrossa on the Florentine border to a point outside the northern gate—the only point where the ground does not fall away steeply outside the walls—and led the water through underground *bottini* until it emerged on the upper rim of the Campo, provoking *tanta allegrezza* that the guilds downed tools and danced in the streets for a fortnight. Nobody would have enjoyed this *festa* and the riposte to Dante more than Cecco, that early case of literary bohemianism, who was so far lacking in proper reverence for the great, though humourless, Florentine that he wrote him three highly impertinent sonnets, the last ending with the line:

Ch'eo so' lo pungiglion, e tu se' 'l bue!
For, Dante, I'm the goad and you're the bull!

It is a pity he did not live to see this triumph. Doubtless only the fact that he was still alive when the *Inferno* was finished saved him from an eternity head downwards in boiling pitch.

Two other aids to the good life deserve a brief mention, the Chains and the Hospital. Outside old houses one sees the iron rings that were used for tethering horses—they are usually held to the wall by delightful little wrought-iron animals, bulls and rams and sea-serpents, and are always worth examining. To these rings, whenever the city's internal peace was threatened by factions of the *grandi* or their mounted myrmidons, heavy chains could be attached from side to side of the street to block the way against sudden charges by bodies of horse. On the other hand such chains did not unduly hinder counter-attacks by the forces of order and social progress on foot. At the present time their employment against motorists and scooters is sadly neglected, but the Hospital of Santa Maria della Scala still fulfils one of the functions for which it was founded in 1090 or earlier. Though at first supervised by the cathedral canons from across the square, it soon became an entirely secular institution staffed by a lay brotherhood, but this independence was not achieved without a struggle. The present building dates from 1298, as a Latin inscription on the wall records, adding that at that time it sheltered three hundred waifs and strays, *et plus*. Like other medieval hospitals it combined with its medical services those of a foundlings' home, an orphanage, an almshouse, and a pilgrims' hostel. These multifarious activities are well shown in Domenico di Bartolo's frescoes in the orthopaedic ward inside, which, though they date from the 1440s, present scenes of overcrowded and chaotic beneficence which must have gone on for centuries before, and for that matter continue today on not entirely dissimilar lines in the ward below them. [*Plate* 31.]

There can be little doubt that this remarkable Hospital performed more good works in Siena with less fuss than did the two orders of friars put together. The latter's large churches, towering over the poor quarters on opposite sides of the town, belong to this period too. The Franciscans began theirs in 1326 in a straightforward style adapted, like Protestant churches, for sermons, and following the rules laid down to this end by the order's chapter general at Narbonne in 1260. There are no aisles; the nave is lit by a plain western rose-window and plain lancets; the roof is of wood, except for some vaulting at the east end. This barn-like, T-shaped church contains little to detain the visitor apart from the frescoes by the two Lorenzetti, already mentioned. The Dominican church across the city is on very similar lines, though begun earlier. There is a large crypt and another vast T-shaped church above, now being most drastically pruned of its Baroque accretions, for which the new stained-glass windows are deemed a suitable substitute. It is visited for St. Catherine's chapel and other sites connected with her. The church's position on the edge of a slowly disintegrating cliff is evidently an inspiration rather than a source of anxiety to St. Catherine's countrymen in the building trade.

A cathedral is always being added to, and in 1284 the task of constructing a west front opposite the Hospital was entrusted to Giovanni Pisano. At the same time he exchanged Pisan for Sienese citizenship. There has been a good deal of learned controversy about exactly what he did and whether his work was subsequently demolished to allow for an extension of the nave westwards, but it is now generally accepted that the lower half of the façade as it stands is his. But it is important to realize that he was not responsible for the remarkable constructions above the cornice at aisle level which makes a strong horizontal division half-way up the façade. These upper embellishments were added nearly a century later.* They dominate the general impression so much that it is a little difficult to appreciate Giovanni Pisano's design, particularly as some of his statues have been transposed at some time and the most weather-beaten removed to the Opera del Duomo where at close range their accentuated poses, meant to be seen forty feet up, look rather odd. French cathedrals crowd their statuary within the shelter of the arches, whereas here the figures are far fewer, and lean out to cast shadows and emphasize points high up in the structure. [*Plates* 11, 27.]

Under the Nine the cathedral went through extraordinary vicissitudes. At the beginning of the *trecento*, a clerestory and vaulting replaced the original timber roof of the nave. The external appearance of the cupola, which had risen clear above the old roof, suffered in the process. Work was also resumed on the east end where, because the ground fell away precipitously, the plan was to build a baptistery at the bottom of the slope and to extend the choir above it. But before the work had got very far, the Sienese architect Lorenzo di Maitano threw doubts on the propriety and safety of what had been done and put forward a much more ambitious plan. This was to build a huge new nave at right angles to the existing one; the latter, with the choir, when finished, would form the transepts of a gigantic cathedral orientated to the north-west instead of to the north-east. It is clear that in the eyes of contemporaries the chief if not the only merit of this proposal was that it would give Siena a larger cathedral than that of Florence. For seventeen years the plan was wisely resisted. Then, in 1339, they made up their minds to attempt it. Another Sienese architect, Lando di Pietro, was fetched from where he was working at Naples and put in charge. As if the scale of the enterprise was not already over-confident, he made the piers of the new nave so recklessly slender that, when most of them had been built, it was found that they could not support the vault above. Italian taste rejected the flying buttress and other external props which alone make this

* See pages 75–76.

kind of building possible. Lando di Pietro knew little of such foreign contraptions and would not sully his drawing-board with them.

There the matter rested, until the shock of the Black Death, cracks in the new fabric, the head-shakings of experts brought in from the more sober city on the Arno, and the fall from power of the Nine combined to induce Siena to abandon the attempt altogether. The graceful, over-bold Gothic piers and light round arches, more suited to an immense loggia than to a vaulted nave, remain to testify to one side of Sienese character. If Dante had lived to see them, he would have been confirmed in his pessimistic estimate of *la gente vana*. But below three of those sweeping arches, in what would have become an aisle, the Opera del Duomo now shelters some of Giovanni Pisano's statues and the more precious *Maestà* of Duccio di Buoninsegna, with other works of his that no one can call vain. And in the tall doorway opening on to the steps that lead to the baptistery, the Sienese arch achieved its culmination. Through this gracious portal of sculptured marble we pass out and down to a meaner and more unhappy age. [*Plate* 30.]

5

Late Medieval Siena as it was

NOTHING IS MORE typical of the late Middle Ages, a contradictory age of flamboyance and decay, than an emperor's visit to Rome. By now the Holy Roman Empire was obsolescent. Gone were the days when a Frederick Barbarossa could hammer Lombard cities into temporary submission. Instead, a fourteenth-century emperor was almost inclined to share other people's doubts concerning his legitimate primacy, unless he had been crowned in Rome. Accordingly he seldom failed to undertake a most vexatious journey for the purpose, lumbering uncomfortably through the Brenner with an inadequate army and a prodigious quantity of luggage and clanking down the peninsula to Rome like a dinosaur to its water-hole. The expenses of this tour could usually be recovered by the sale of knighthoods to the more snobbish Italian citizens and of charters, decorated with the imperial autograph and seal, to the more impressionable municipalities, for jurists still upheld the emperor's theoretical sovereignty, just as Rome was still the theoretical seat of the papacy, although the French pope and his cardinals had for some time been enjoying the more bracing air of Avignon. Situated on the main road southwards, Siena was the obvious choice for an emperor's rest before the final spurt to the capital, or for a rallying point after pestilence or the volatile population of the Trastevere had driven him out. A hundred years after Montaperti, Ghibelline memories in Siena had acquired the romantic harmlessness of Jacobite memories in Edinburgh at the time of the brothers Sobieski Stuart, and the Sienese could be relied on to receive an emperor with enthusiasm, extract some honorific privileges from him and send him on his way when he outstayed his welcome, which being a German he usually did.

It says something for the vitality of these people that, less than seven years after the Black Death, they were prepared to enter into the spirit of one of these visits and even to convert a charade into a revolution. The rule of the Nine, who expected things to remain as they were after such a cataclysm, had become impossible. A monopoly of power and economic privilege by rich wool merchants was out of keeping with the changed state of the labour market, and their personal pretentions were unbearable. The Nine organized a civic welcome for Charles IV of Luxemburg and his empress, but barely had the august cortège reached the Palazzo Salimbeni before the storm broke. Agents of the Piccolomini raised the cry, 'Death to the Nine!' Other patrician families and their retainers joined in the clamour, the guildsmen and wool-workers appeared in arms, starting up out of their hovels in the low-lying ward of the Caterpillar and pouring through the wynds into the Campo, where they prepared to assault the government in their palace. Charles mediated, the Nine abdicated. Deserted by all, they fled to avoid personal violence while the populace sacked and burnt their houses. Twelve councillors from the *popolo* replaced the Nine, together with a short-lived advisory body of patricians. The revolution was celebrated with a *festa* so rapturous that the emperor, conferring honours right and left, knighted a number of quite humble citizens by mistake and against their own will. More helpfully he granted the University imperial recognition, which it had hitherto lacked, and which was now felt to be desirable.

When the dust had been laid Siena found itself under a government of Twelve, all of the lower middle class. It appears that the Twelve showed more of the failings than of the virtues of this layer of society. Nor had they even borne the brunt of the recent uprising. The subject towns in the *contado* thought even less of them than did their fellow-citizens. Montepulciano transferred its allegiance to Perugia, kicking off a war in the Val di Chiana. Rather surprisingly Siena had the best of it, recovering Montepulciano and taking Cortona, far beyond the traditional frontiers. But this war was expensive and saw the increasing use of mercenaries, of which whole units were hired for the occasion. These mercenary 'free companies' were often composed of non-Italians; when not engaged by some city-state, they raided different territories impartially, and in most cases had to be ignominiously bought off. On one occasion Siena hit back. The *capitano di guerra*, Orsini, disregarded his express orders from the over-cautious Twelve and inflicted a memorable defeat on the Breton Company of the Hat. But next year the Company of the Star appeared in its place, followed by the yet more formidable White Company under Sir John Hawkwood, the greatest *condottiere* of his day. He routed a Sienese army and exacted a fat sum before he went.*

Faced with plots from all sides, the government of the Twelve became a tyranny. 'And the Signori Dodici entered into great fear of the air and appointed police captains in every *terzo* of the city with many soldiers under them; and to these officials they gave ample authority to behead whosoever should cough against them. . . .'†

The great virtue of the Sienese was that, unlike the peoples of many Italian cities, they never put up with this sort of thing for long, and in 1368 the *grandi* temporarily abandoned their own feuds and expelled the Twelve with no more than a show of force. But a purely patrician government was not to be borne either, and in the course of the next four months four further revolutions convulsed the unfortunate city. First the people, the Salimbeni (playing a lone hand) and the imperial vicar drove out the nobles and set

* Sir John Hawkwood or *Messer Giovanni Acuto*, originally of Sible Hedingham in Essex, spent the latter years of a long and eventful career in the service of Florence, where his monument, a *trompe l'œil* equestrian painting by Paolo Uccello, can be seen in the cathedral.

† Muratori, *Rerum Italicarum Scriptores*, XV, 192, E, quoted by Schevill, p. 218.

up a council in which three *monti* or parties were represented, including for the first time the working class or *popolo minuto*. Next the *popolo minuto* seized the Palace and excluded the others. After more disturbances they re-admitted adherents of the Nine and the Twelve as minority groups in their government, which took the name of the *Riformatori*. Finally Charles IV, once more the guest of the Salimbeni, lent himself to the intrigues of that egregious house and tried to overthrow the new government. It was believed that he intended to dismember the *contado* and even to sell the city to the pope, whose legate arrived with another armed body to add to the confusion. The bells were rung *a stormo*, the people rose once more, an unnerving uproar filled the narrow streets, the emperor's cavalry were defeated in the Campo and the Banchi di Sopra with four hundred killed. Charles, now besieged in the Palazzo Salimbeni, was possibly as confused as the reader by Sienese politics. He lost his head, blamed the Salimbeni, wept on whatever necks presented themselves, appointed the scornful *Riformatori* his vicars, scattered pardons, privileges, and letters patent in all directions, pocketed whatever fees were offered him for such documents, and thankfully left the turbulent city for good.

The Sienese specialize in such scenes of uninhibited chaos, nowadays happily transferred to a less lethal plane. They even have their own local word for this phenomenon —*un trafuglío*.*

For the next seventeen years the city was governed by the *Riformatori*, a council of Fifteen composed of eight of the *popolo minuto*, four *dodicini*, and three *noveschi* or, in modern terms, of eight working-class, four petty-bourgeois, and three upper-middle-class representatives. Only the *grandi* were left out. This is perhaps the first 'popular front' or left-wing coalition government in Western history, at any rate the first effective one. It was inaugurated not with a carnival such as had hailed the advent of the Twelve, but with a solemn Mass of Reconciliation in the cathedral, which goes to show how far the cultural overtones of Continental bourgeois and working-class movements have changed since then. Such nuances apart, the idea of a coalition, with the parties represented in proportions roughly corresponding to their numerical strength in the city, is quite clearly a notable advance on the one-party régimes that had gone before. After some Florentine mediation, the great families too were reconciled with the state, being admitted to all but the key posts. A new militant organization of the *popolo* was founded to uphold the constitution. Its insignia, a white lion rampant on a red field, can still be seen on public buildings and elsewhere, beside the black-and-white shield of the commune, and recalls a polity that was a great deal more democratic than most medieval states.

To us it may seem curious that Siena did not adopt the one-man-one-vote basis of democracy as we understand it, instead of juggling somewhat arbitrarily with the number of places held by each *monte* in the government. To this a medieval Sienese might answer that we today, with far longer experience behind us, still accept considerable anomalies in our own electoral system in order to obtain a more effective government. If he were a philosopher he might add that the Middle Ages believed with Aristotle that

* The standard Italian *tafferúglio* has a weaker meaning.

political justice does not imply equality, but rather right proportion according to merit. Viewed from this lofty though question-begging angle, a Sienese coalition approached closer to their representative ideal than a modern British government, seldom supported by more than a bare majority of the electorate, does to ours.

The most valid criticism of the Sienese in politics is that they did not learn to trust each other enough, or to behave so as to encourage such trust. Nor, as has been mentioned already, did they have the insight to extend full citizenship to the peasantry and to those who lived in the small towns within the *contado*. Even in the idealized fresco of *Good Government*, the peasants look surly. The city-state could never jump over its own town walls.

This troubled period coincides with the life of Siena's most famous citizen. St. Catherine was born a year before the Black Death and died late in the epoch of the *Riformatori*. By any standards she was a quite extraordinary woman. She made a prodigious impression upon her contemporaries, and in Siena today her fame completely eclipses that of several other local saints with whose lives the modern Northerner finds himself a good deal more in sympathy. [*Plate* 34.]

Caterina Benincasa was the youngest but one of an enormous family—of twenty-five, according to her monkish biographer. She grew up in the steep, strong-smelling alleys of one of those industrial hollows on the edge of the city, not the wool-carders' district of the Caterpillar but the dyers' and tanners' ward of the Goose. Her father, a master dyer, belonged to the inner councils of that powerful but uninspiring faction, the *dodicini*. On the crest above their street the Dominican friars had built the severe brick church, designed for preaching to the proletariat, whose tall terracotta bulk still dominates that humble quarter. From early childhood it dominated Catherine's life.

At the age of six she saw a heavenly vision in the sky above that church. At seven she took a vow of virginity. As she grew up, nothing her family could do could make her behave like other girls. Once an elder sister persuaded her to have her hair done; afterwards she did much penance for this sin. Despite everyone's misgivings, she insisted on joining a Dominican lay order, although it was intended for widows and she was only fifteen. Unlike other members of the sisterhood, who were meant to give some service to religion while leading their normal lives, she invariably wore the order's black-and-white habit, turned her room at home into a cell, cut herself off from everyone and only left the house to worship in San Domenico. Moderation always seemed to her a second best.

For three years she lived withdrawn from the world in meditations, trances, and visionary ecstasies, many of which have been described at length for posterity in the wholly inadequate language of words. The pious and the psychologist find the most significant of them the vision in which she was married to Christ with a ring and heavenly witnesses, and a later one when she exchanged hearts with her Bridegroom. After such experiences she re-emerged into the life of the city and began that arduous and devoted service to the sick (accompanied by some peculiar acts of self-mortification) which was the second facet of her complex nature.

So far all this is the commonplace of medieval sainthood in its extreme form, and we may pass over the details, though not without some uneasy wonder at an aspect of human personality which cannot flourish equally in our modern subtopia, beset by professionalized social services, school attendance officers, and common sense. We now come to a larger stumbling-block. A side to St. Catherine's character which repels us as much as it appealed to some of her contemporaries is her emotional preoccupation with blood. This was doubtless due in the first place to the crudities of popular medieval preaching, but it went far beyond that. Blood, any blood, had some abnormal meaning for her. She was constantly speaking and writing of it. On her death-bed she cried out the word repeatedly. The most curious episode in this connexion was when a young man whom she had visited in prison was condemned to death. From the gaol, where she had restored his faith, she accompanied him to the scaffold and, kneeling beside the block, caught his head as it fell from the executioner's blow. 'Then,' she wrote, 'my soul rested in peace and stillness and in so great an aroma of blood, that I could not bear to wash off the blood that had spurted over me.' So rapturous a reaction to human blood, however explained, seems an unwholesome trait in a young woman.

Her contemporaries, on the whole, did not think so. By the time she was twenty she already had a group of devoted disciples, both men and women, whose dependence upon her was complete and touching. But it is worth noting that others, equally sincere in their religion, rejected her. Although several of the hermits of Lecceto were among her closest friends and followers, the contemporary historian of Lecceto, Fra Filippo, never mentions her or them in his biographical collection, the *Assempri*. Nor did she ever come in contact with that other Sienese saint whose life overlapped with hers, the Blessed Giovanni Colombini, a rich merchant and former member of the Nine who left his counting-house in later life to found the *Gesuati*, a small order enthusiastically devoted to genuine poverty. Clearly not only the twentieth century has found St. Catherine difficult.

What makes her live again for us, and lifts her out of the run of medieval saints, is her correspondence. Nearly four hundred of her letters have been preserved. In them she reveals yet another aspect of herself, that of an exceptionally strong-minded and forthright woman, of a sort nowadays more often found in Anglo-Saxon than in Latin countries. Unlike St. Francis of Assisi, who was humble and diffident in argument, this woman never doubts for a moment that she is right. Though she writes of herself with exaggerated humility, her letters are rebukes and commands, forcefully directed towards the moral improvement of the persons addressed and making painfully few concessions to human weakness or to the arts of persuasion. On those already more or less aware of their own shortcomings their effect must have been electric, but anyone who sincerely disagreed with her opinion can only have found her letters shrill and unconvincing. Some of those she addressed to hermits leading a consecrated life, in which she tells them how to do it better, must have sorely tested the recipients' holiness. One of these hermits was a Cambridge man, William Flete, who lived in the ilex woods of Lecceto near Siena, and whom she repeatedly rebuked for what in her Italian eyes were his outstanding faults of reserve, desire for solitude, and unperturbed independent judgement. Other letters treat with gentle but telling severity an immense variety of people, such as quarrelsome priests (to whom she expresses her surprise that the earth has not yet swallowed them up), mothers who are too affectionate, little girls who seek praise from other people, and frivolous widows who go to weddings, dress smartly, and keep their faces anointed, instead of mourning for ever like the turtle-dove.

As time goes on, more and more of these letters are written to statesmen in order to put them right on questions of the day. Starting with appeals to take part in another crusade, such as that which she made to Sir John Hawkwood 'since you delight so much in fighting', she was soon involved in a comprehensive attempt to restore church and state to conformity with her exalted medieval ideal. It was a desperate counter-attack against the waning of the Middle Ages. Her political attitude was one of extreme papalism, as out of date by then as Dante's imperialist creed had become sixty years earlier, and was complicated by the fact that when addressing 'Christ on earth' at Avignon she regarded herself as speaking on behalf of 'Christ in heaven'. While condemning as sacrilege the slightest opposition to the governors of the Papal States, she tells the pope that they are 'incarnate demons'. She instructs him on his duties and urges him to make reforms, after which he must launch the long-delayed crusade. He should appoint more virtuous men as cardinals and a better new head of the Dominicans, 'because the order has run too wild'. Writing to the king of France, she urges him 'to do God's will and mine'.

These letters paved the way for a diplomatic mission which she now undertook, and which brought her life to its climax. It was the year 1376. The States of the Church, fast expanding and now encircling the Florentine frontiers on two sides, had banned food exports to that city at a time of famine there. This and other threatening acts, which had more to do with power-politics than with Christianity, provoked the Florentines to elect a more vigorous government, splendidly named the Eight of War, and to encourage rebellion in the Papal States. Aided by Florence, a large number of recently subjugated cities rose against the Temporal Power. The pope, from Avignon, replied with that old weapon an interdict, a little rusty but still effective against foreign trade. Before things could get any worse, the more moderate party in Florence arranged for Catherine to go to Avignon and mediate on their city's behalf. She, of course, had not been inactive in this crisis. On her own account she had already done her best to persuade Lucca, Pisa, and other towns not to join the Florentines. The Eight of War can hardly have expected her to act with the discretion or even the loyalty of an ordinary ambassador. If they had fully realized what she was up to, they might not have sent her, and if she had foreseen all the consequences she would scarcely have gone. But send her they did, and soon, undismayed by the difficulties of fourteenth-century travel, the saint and her band of disciples came to the gay though wind-swept city on the Rhône.

To most Italians, whether high-minded like Dante and Petrarch or those more interested in patronage and pickings, the residence of the popes at Avignon was a 'Babylonish captivity'. Expenses had risen and the Curia's financial expedients had become widely unpopular. Simony was open and fortune-hunters came to Avignon in droves. In matters of diplomacy and politics these seven French popes followed the wishes of the king of France, though on this score, in seventy years, they had only committed one unforgivable crime, the atrocious injustice to the Templars. Their court lived with rather less austerity than the times expected of it; in fact the vast fortified palace, chaotically planned but luxurious inside, fairly seethed with pastrycooks, cellarers, falconers, and cardinals' nieces, though modern historians discount Petrarch's more lurid accounts of what went on inside it. But the papacy at Avignon was by no means wholly ignoble. It had improved if over-centralized its administration, tried to reform some of the monastic orders, helped to found some new universities, protected the Jews from persecution. organized missions overseas, and striven hard though fruitlessly for a crusade. If it was in the French king's pocket, to Frenchmen this seemed the most appropriate pocket to be in. And its non-political weaknesses were not the fault of its location. As has often been pointed out, it was not the provincial town of Avignon that corrupted the papal court, but the other way round.

Gregory XI had already perused five of Catherine's outspoken letters with other messages 'from Christ crucified and from me', exhorting him to revise his policies and mend his cardinals' ways of life. It is to his credit that he now received the Florentine ambassadress in that great hall which her countryman Simone Martini had decorated. Perhaps, on the diplomatic level, Gregory knew what he was doing, for soon she was writing back to the Florentines to remind them of the obedience they owed him and extending it from the spiritual to the political sphere. They should feel grief for the wrong they had done him; they should humble themselves before him and should stop taxing the clergy. If he punished them, it was the act of a father, done for their own good. Gregory himself demanded that Florence should break with its allies and pay a vast indemnity. The Florentines obstinately rejected peace on these terms and disowned their envoy. However, if Gregory thought he had got the better of this mission, he was wrong. She was aiming much higher.

It was the crowning achievement of her life. In passionate harangues and, when she was denied audience, in further letters, she urged Gregory to return to his rightful place in Rome, trusting in his spiritual authority rather than in his military establishment. 'Take heed,' she advised him, 'not to come with armed men, but like a meek lamb.' The unfortunate Gregory, who had previously endured the similar demands and revelations of St. Bridget of Sweden,* finally yielded to the arguments of this second prophetess, or perhaps more to certain practical considerations—recent incursions of bandit armies had made Avignon, too, unsafe, and the Romans were threatening to take another pope if Gregory did not come back to them. Naturally the 'incarnate demons' strongly opposed the move. The French king did not like it, and the French cardinals were frankly aghast at the thought of exchanging their delightful mansions for the damp

* In St. Bridget's case modern Catholic scholarship concludes that she 'intermixed with the gifts she received from heaven a great part of her own burning imagination'. Might not the same be said of St. Catherine?

palazzi of the Eternal City, surrounded by murderous nobles and a wildly undisciplined population. But their duty was made clear to them and in a subdued spirit the Curia took the road, although Gregory's old father made a scene on the doorstep and the mule which His Holiness first mounted utterly refused to move in the direction of Marseilles.

On reaching Genoa the cardinals, their perfidy increased by recent sea-sickness, almost persuaded the vacillating pontiff to slip back to Avignon. But St. Catherine appeared again, a figure of fate, and strengthened his resolution. On the resumed voyage two of the French cardinals were shipwrecked. Contrary to popular Sienese legend—as shown, for instance, in a fresco in the Hospital of the Scala by Matteo di Giovanni—she did not accompany them, though Letter 252 reached them on the way there and propelled them onwards. One is sad that she missed the triumphal entry into Rome, the visible reward of her faith and courage. And just as regrettably, on the human plane, her faith was misplaced.

Gregory, from motives of common prudence, had not taken all her good advice. He had assembled ample forces of mercenaries and had engaged the highly competent Sir John Hawkwood. Within three weeks of the Holy Father's return to Rome his army perpetrated a treacherous massacre of civilians at Cesena on a scale that shocked even that case-hardened age. After this start the government of the Papal States, whenever it had the power, continued on firm lines up to 1870. Neither this lamb nor subsequent lambs were meek. Catherine's last letters to Gregory show her disillusion; she implores him to make peace whatever the cost and to seek to win souls rather than cities. Modern experience has proved her right. The power of the Holy See does not depend on armed possession of central Italy.

Catherine spent a few peaceful months turning the ruined castle of Belcaro, just outside Siena, into a monastery. It had been given her by a rich convert. In another brief interlude she dictated her *Dialogue*, a treatise containing some of the essence of her intense, mystical religion, written 'with a desire to know and to follow the truth in a more virile way'. In between, politics claimed her again, first a feud in the Val d'Orcia to be reconciled, and then once more the insoluble contradictions of the Temporal Power.

Florence was still at war with Gregory, and Catherine went there as his envoy to make peace. She became involved with the rich reactionaries of the *Parte Guelfa*, who used her ingenuous support of the more clerical faction in Florence to sanctify their aim of proscribing all their political opponents. During a popular rising provoked by their unfairness, a mob burst into her garden. To her great dismay they refused her a martyrdom. Peace came through the pressure of events rather than through any activities of hers, and she left the city hurriedly to avoid giving rise to another hostile demonstration. Truth is a complicated thing.

Worse was to come. Gregory XI had died. With his last breath he warned those around his death-bed 'to beware of all those persons, whether men or women, who under the guise of religion proclaimed their own infatuated visions, for he himself had been led astray by such'. Gibbon, in one of those Augustan passages which he reserves for the Church's misfortunes, describes what happened next. The French cardinals were in a majority, and by electing a French pope might hope to get back to Avignon, but

> 'The licentiousness of the seditious Romans was inflamed by a sense of their privileges, and the danger of a second emigration. The conclave was intimidated by the shouts, and encompassed by the arms, of 30,000 rebels; the bells of the Capitol and St. Peter's rang an alarm; "Death, or an Italian pope!' was the universal cry; the same threat was repeated by the twelve bannerets or chiefs of the quarters, in the form of charitable advice; some preparations were made for burning the obstinate cardinals; and had they chosen a Transalpine subject, it is probable that they would never have departed alive from the Vatican.'

Thus constrained, the French cardinals joined at least in the outward form of electing an Italian, Urban VI. If they hoped he would prove a nonentity, they never made a greater mistake. He was autocratic, bad-tempered, and anti-French. It was noticed that when anyone contradicted him, his face became like a burning lamp. His behaviour antagonized even many Italians. The cardinals fled, declared Urban's election void because unfree, and elected a combative member of the French party instead. He took the name of Clement VII and presently, after military reverses, returned to Avignon. Beside the support of France he gained that of Scotland, the Spanish kingdoms, Southern Italy, Savoy, and Cyprus. The other, less individual countries of Europe plumped for Urban VI. The Great Schism lasted for thirty-seven years. Clement and his successors are nowadays reckoned in Rome as antipopes, but that is only a convenient historical fiction. At the time, at least as many men of weight, sincerity, and learning were found on the Clementine side as on the Urbanist.*

In this unhappy controversy St. Catherine took as active and partisan a part as her worn-out health permitted. In her black-and-white view of things, Clement and his supporters were just a new and worse variety of 'incarnate demons'. She spent the last seventeen months of her life in a Rome which was at first militarily divided between the two factions. Her courage and her fiery support of Urban strengthened the resolve of a man who, this time, needed no strengthening. In due course his second batch of prelates 'discovered the features of the tyrant, who could walk in his garden and recite his breviary, while he heard from an adjacent chamber six cardinals groaning on the rack'. Catherine addressed letters to cities, to monasteries, to princes both friendly and hostile. She got Urban to summon all the hermits she knew to come to Rome and demonstrate in his favour, and was furious when the Englishman William Flete refused to leave his wood for this pontifical whirlpool. 'There are woods here too,' she told him, glancing through her visionary eye-slits at the treeless Campagna. But it was now clear, even to

* The most conscientious inquiry into the issue was that conducted by the kingdom of Castile, which pronounced for Clement. St. Vincent Ferrer worked for and welcomed this decision. The Council of Constance, which eventually ended the Schism, avoided giving a verdict on which line of popes had been legitimate.

unworldly minds, that the return from Avignon had been premature, and poor Catherine's passionate views on the problems of the Holy See commanded less respect.

Nothing daunted, she hurled a bombshell of a letter at the three neutral-minded Italian cardinals who had tacitly consented to Clement's election. 'Fools, worthy of a thousand deaths! . . . Liars and idolaters! . . .'—and added that they were even more guilty than the French cardinals, who had the excuse of their nationalism, whereas 'humanly speaking, Christ on earth is an Italian, and so are you'. She tried to get the Florentines to pay their indemnity to Urban. She incited a Hungarian army to attack the queen of Naples. She sought to moderate Urban's irascibility. Seriously ill, she had a vision that the Ship of the Church, which she saw in Giotto's mosaic in St. Peter's, was laid on her shoulders and crushed her to the ground. Exulting in *tanti dolci tormenti corporali*, she died, aged only thirty-three. She was buried in Santa Maria sopra Minerva, the only Gothic church in Rome, built over a temple to a militant goddess.

Today her countrymen have forgotten her disastrous interventions in church politics and remember her calls for peace and her active, unsparing love.

. . . . .

Meanwhile, what had happened to that promising popular government in Siena, the *Riformatori*?

Successful rebels who achieve power by something less than an outright victory often have to meet trouble from their own extremists. The wool-carders down by the Porta Ovile had formed a revolutionary ginger-group. From the name of their ward or *contrada* it was known as the League of the Caterpillar. In their simple view the revolution of 1368 had been betrayed by including class enemies in the coalition. Driven to desperation by long experience of hard-faced guild-masters and the sight of their own hungry families, the League of the Caterpillar ran many-footed into the Palazzo and threw out their opponents; they also broke into grain-stores. This was in 1371, some years before the corresponding rising of the *Ciompi* in Florence. A combination of army officers and the lower bourgeoisie, depressingly suggestive of Italy in 1922, planned a counter-stroke. Although their plot went wrong and they were unable to seize a gate and let in the feudal levies of the Salimbeni, who needless to say were in the conspiracy, they started a wholesale massacre in the wool-carders' quarter, slaughtering the ill-armed workers and their families, until the government, helped by the more responsible elements, rallied enough forces to restore order.

After the leading officers involved in this affair had been executed and the wretched *dodicini* turned out of the government, the *Riformatori* held office for another fourteen years. They were now an overwhelmingly working-class régime. Such a government, lasting so long, is a unique phenomenon in the fourteenth century, although there were similar social movements in other economically advanced cities, for example in the Flemish towns and in Nuremberg, Cologne, and Florence. But in all these cases the day of the under-dogs was very much shorter, owing to inter-guild rivalries and to the greater strength of the merchant plutocracy.

In Siena the *Riformatori*, far from liquidating the upper classes, do not seem to have aimed at anything more drastic than a fair deal for small craftsmen and employees. They carried out a reform of the national debt, converting it into negotiable loan stock at a sensibly low rate of interest. It was secured on the salt monopoly and on taxes paid by the huge sheep farms of the Maremma. In the course of centuries the body administering this loan developed into the *Monte dei Paschi di Siena*, one of the great banks of Italy, with its head office now in the Palazzo Salimbeni.

Their worst troubles were outside the walls. They had to conduct a long struggle with the Salimbeni, now exiled, in the south of the *contado*, which was also repeatedly devastated by wandering mercenaries and bandits. All this drained the treasury dry. Finally their army was defeated by Hawkwood in the Papal States, and Florence forestalled them in a take-over bid for Arezzo. In 1385 there came the inevitable armed rising, this time of the burghers led by the Saracini. This counter-revolution was hand in glove with the restored oligarchs of Florence, who had had the scare of their lives from their own *Ciompi*. The slogan, 'Long live peace!' divided the plebs and secured victory. After all was over, the new government drove the hard core of Caterpillar militants into exile. Four thousand left the city, which soon found the loss of so much skilled labour less easy to replace than that of a few nobles. 'And I the chronicler,' wrote Agnolo di Tura or his successor, 'who am not of the party of the *Riformatori*, judged that it was a bad thing to have done, for in this way they harmed and impoverished the city of Siena by driving out in batches more than four thousand good workers who were citizens of our city, and of whom not one in six ever came back.'

6

Late Medieval Siena as it is

THE YEAR 1357, following close on the revolution that ushered in the petty-bourgeois Twelve, saw two artistic casualties. One was the attempt to transform the cathedral; as already mentioned, this was the year in which that rash enterprise was finally given up. The other casualty, a sadder one, was a Greek goddess. Some dozen years back a marble Aphrodite had been unearthed while digging water-conduits in the city. The beautiful thing had been brought in triumph to the Campo and set up above the new fountain—not yet della Quercia's, of course—amid general admiration and rejoicing. Ambrogio Lorenzetti had drawn it, and on seeing his sketch a century later the sculptor Ghiberti had no hesitation in declaring that the original had been carved by Lysippus. Whatever we may think of this attribution, and Siena's insignificance in Classical times speaks against it, the statue was obviously a work of merit. But now, in the aftermath of the plague, some superstitious grocer in the new council asserted that recent calamities were a divine judgement for doing honour to a pagan idol. His colleagues agreed unanimously, the immodest deity was taken down and broken, and the pieces were buried with thoughtful malevolence over the Florentine border. If only it had been found a hundred years later!

The Sienese turned back to less risky varieties of sacred art. The Black Death, which killed both the Lorenzetti, spared Barna da Siena. Art-historians speak of his debt to Simone Martini and even to Duccio, but to the layman little of this is apparent. In spirit he is poles apart. For their refined, elegant serenity he substituted a most violent expressionism. His saints are tortured with remorse and his soldiers are thugs. Gross emotions and plebeian faces stare at us from the frescoes at San Gimignano. Barna has lifted the lid off the sufferings of the common people, as he saw them during the plague and the social ferment that followed it. It has been said that his figures look like actors, so packed with drama are these scenes, but Barna's raw images must surely have been derived from an experience more direct than watching passion-plays.

All the same, it seems beyond a coincidence that there are so few expressionist pictures in Siena itself, at least until Matteo di Giovanni in the late *quattrocento*. Sienese taste, which was tenaciously conservative over a long period, appears to have frowned on expressionism and probably felt it was vulgar. Subjects like the Last Judgement are relatively rare. The two most powerful Sienese expressionists, Pietro Lorenzetti and Barna, had to move to places like Assisi and San Gimignano before they could let themselves go.

No sooner had Barna been killed by a fall from his scaffolding than a fresh phenomenon appears in this versatile community, that of the artist in revolutionary politics. Andrea Vanni, Niccolo di Buonaccorso, and Bartolo di Fredi, the three best Sienese painters of the late *trecento*, were all of them active supporters of the *Riformatori*, and the first for certain joined in the street-fighting of 1368. Painters who take part in revolutions are often content with some heroic but not very practical gesture, like Courbet's when he incited a group of bystanders to demolish the Colonne Vendôme in 1871. But the Sienese *fédéraux* were victorious, as we have seen, and their régime lasted for seventeen years, in the course of which these three artists took a leading part in public affairs. Their political sympathies have a curiously nineteenth-century ring about them, and it would be interesting to know how they originated in such different surroundings. As for political ability, they had more than the Impressionists; Andrea and Niccolo were several times members of the government, both Andrea and Bartolo filled the post of *capitano del popolo*, Bartolo became governor of Massa Marittima, and Andrea was latterly ambassador at Avignon and Naples.

Perhaps on account of too many public engagements, more probably because patronage and public taste confined them to outworn themes, these politically conscious artists have left us nothing first-rate. Bartolo di Fredi's principal work, like Barna's, is at San Gimignano; his frescoes are overcrowded but very much alive. Andrea Vanni was a friend of St. Catherine's; he received three of her intimidating letters and painted her portrait, which is his best-known work. Niccolo di Buonaccorso left nothing much in Siena; there is a picture of his in London. There are several lesser figures like Luca di Tomè and, towards the end of the century, Paolo di Giovanni Fei, Andrea di Bartolo, and his better-known brother Taddeo, none of them very original, or with much to say to us today. [*Plate* 34.]

It is now after 1400, and we are up against the Sienese painters of the *quattrocento*. They present a problem in more ways than one. The Renaissance overran Siena's artistic territories at very different speeds. Sculpture had fallen before Jacopo della Quercia's attack by about 1420, and in the 1460s the Piccolomini fifth column let in Renaissance architects from Florence who swept all that field before them. But in the sector of painting the defences held out. The Sienese panel-painters obstinately refused to emerge from their traditional stronghold and to make a whole-hearted attempt at the illusory conquest of nature and space. They clung to their aethereal sacred subjects and to many of their old techniques, only slightly modified as time went on. For instance they often used gold backgrounds long after they had become out of date elsewhere. What Renaissance elements crept in were for the most part mere fashionable furnishings, such as the extravagant would-be Roman architecture that some of them pointlessly introduced into pictures that would have been better without it. If they painted with greater delicacy, it was only to make their dream-world still more dream-like. The realism and geometry that stood behind the Florentine Renaissance could make no progress here. This is the more peculiar in that several of these painters were also sculptors, Vecchietta and Francesco di Giorgio in particular. Yet nothing could be less sculptural than their painting. In fact, the old aesthetic double vision had come back.

Since these *quattrocento* painters rejected the Renaissance spirit and most of its techniques, clinging instead to a belated medievalism, they belong to the present chapter rather than to a later one. But it is easier to classify their pictures than to like them. Even the best of them seem rather odd. One wearies of the visionary motifs that, through repetition, lose their wonder. One's taste is cloyed by a treatment which becomes smoother and weaker, with figures in flattish modelling against still flatter backgrounds, a treatment which at its worst suggests bas-reliefs in icing-sugar. That uncongenial travelling-companion, one's Northern puritanism, asserts itself, complaining that there is something *fin-de-siècle* and unhealthy about the output of this little hothouse.

These reactions are not quite fair, certainly not to the best individuals of the first half of the century. Sassetta in particular paints delightfully. The rhythm of his line and the intense luminosity of his colours show him as a direct descendant of Duccio and Simone Martini. His work has been scattered; the best-known picture is at Chantilly, others are in London and America. He is badly represented in the Siena Gallery, but four of his exquisite little pictures glow like fireflies among the stately grandeurs in the Palazzo Chigi-Saracini. They must be seen.

Sano di Pietro possessed some of the same qualities, but was more innocent and very much less imaginative. His traditionalist work made a strong appeal to the general public of his day, with the unfortunate result that the assistants in his bottega turned out Madonnas for local consumption like hens in a battery turning out eggs. His smaller pictures are pleasanter than his big polyptychs; No. 262 gives a naïve glimpse of shepherds in the *creta* country, their black-and-white flock packed into a sheepfank. And the best of his larger works have more merit than is generally allowed.

Giovanni di Paolo dreams of holy men stepping forward into eccentric landscapes and strange perspectives. There is a good example in London. At Siena (No. 206) he has placed his queer Madonna in front of a grove of orange trees and given her the curve of the globe for an additional halo; the little landscape behind her head, with its hills and plains and cities, is a charming piece of unreality. And his *Last Judgement* (No. 172) is a most effective decoration, in which the straight verticals of the orange trees and embracing figures in Paradise contrast well with the honeycomb of fiery grottoes and writhing (but not grossly tortured) shapes in Hell. [*Plate* 37.]

In the 1440s Domenico di Bartolo decided to let in some fresh air from Florence. On the basis of some studies there he revived the technique of fresco-painting, which the Sienese had neglected latterly, and introduced a massive, naturalistic style. His series of frescoes in the Hospital bring the life of that institution and the horrors of a communal nursery forcibly to one's attention. Such scenes of beggars being clothed, foundlings given a bath, and nubile orphan lasses provided with dowries, set in halls restlessly decorated in the Sienese style, are necessarily over-full of activities and figures, but it must be confessed that a Florentine would have given more shape to the whole. Perhaps because they were not outstanding examples of their kind, Domenico di Bartolo's frescoes did not deflect other Sienese painters from their panel-painting or from their unearthliness. It is about here that people of only limited sensibility give up. The writer confesses that, in spite of Mr. Pope-Hennessy,* he wanders more and more disconsolately through this part of the Gallery, past Vecchietta, Matteo di Giovanni, Benvenuto di Giovanni, Francesco di Giorgio, Fungai, and Cozzarelli, past all these saintly yearnings, beatific visions, insubstantial charades, and nasty little martyrdoms with nutmeg-scrapers, only pulled up in his tracks now and then by some detail of local landscape or some piece of anti-realistic genius, such as the weirdly distorted perspective in No. 277 (an *Annunciation* by Francesco di Giorgio) with a little whatnot or lectern that would feel at home in a picture by Braque.† [*Plate* 31.]

Against all this, Matteo di Giovanni's *Massacres of the Innocents*, one in the Servi church, another in Sant' Agostino, and yet another on the Duomo pavement, stand out as an unpleasant island of sadism and another brief relapse into a more naturalistic style. The gloating older children, who did not themselves qualify as victims and are watching from above, are an ingeniously loathsome touch, and the oriental perpetrators suggest that these pictures are a reaction to the sack of Otranto by the Turks in 1480, which caused a considerable shock throughout Italy.

Towards the end of the century the last of these painters, Neroccio dei Landi, evidently felt too that Sienese art was getting out of hand, and returned to Duccio for fresh inspiration. The result, added to the mannerisms of his age, is a queer, ultra-refined beauty verging on the decadent. His long-necked Madonnas, again strikingly feline, mark the close of a great tradition. [*Plate* 36.]

It is no accident that all this output of painting in fifteenth-century Siena was not balanced by any comparable achievement in literature. It is exactly what one would expect of a small, economically static mercantile republic before the ages of printing and mass education. Literature in Renaissance Italy, completely dominated by Classical studies, was the preserve of a learned élite and depended on highbrow princely patronage, whereas painting was much closer to the people, being related to the ordinary craftsman's own abilities, financially within the means of middle-class pockets or guild funds, and more directly emotional in its appeal. These social factors joined forces with a certain lack of intellectual curiosity, discernible in the Sienese temperament as early as the time when their artists rejected Giotto, and in the long run their greatest innate weakness. And so they were creative only in the visual arts.

In this field their enthusiasm knew no bounds. It went to the length of employing leading artists of the day to paint commemorative pictures on the covers of treasury blue books and the annual accounts of the inland revenue department. The practice dates

* See his *Sienese Quattrocento Painting* (Phaidon, 1947).

† Francesco di Giorgio was a versatile Renaissance architect and knew all about perspective. In this picture he must have rejected it on purpose, to convey the surprise of the message.

from as early as 1258. These *Tavolette della Biccherna e della Gabella*, now shown in the Palazzo Piccolomini among the civic archives, are a fascinating series of social documents, occasionally of some artistic merit, more often just pleasantly illustrative. The earliest display the heraldry or the portraits of city treasurers (*camarlinghi*) whom we see cautiously counting out money behind their desks—at first they are monks from San Galgano and later laymen. Later *tavolette* comment allegorically on various public events. There is a good one of 1468 showing where the money goes, to the citizens in peacetime and to loudly-dressed mercenary brass-hats in war. St. Catherine's pacifism, unpractical and one-sided though it was, made a great appeal to the generations that followed her. There must have been a frightful financial scandal in 1451; Sano di Pietro shows the treasurer demonstratively washing his hands, while the Virgin flies through the air to protect her city. And so on through the record of earthquakes, papal visitations, sieges, and deliverances.

Any stranger found walking in the north-western quarter of the city is assumed by the kindly inhabitants to be looking for St. Catherine's house and will be conducted thither, by force if necessary, in order to be shown the staircase up which she was levitated at a tender age. Such houses are often disappointing, and the visitor with limited time and sufficient determination may perhaps be recommended to evade this particular duty. At least he should not be made to go there more than once. But the ability to reply with a polite but convincing vernacular negative to the question, '*Vuole vedere la casa di Santa Caterina?*' is essential if one wants to explore the rest of this picturesque area, which includes some cavernous streets, San Domenico, and the Fontebranda.

St. Catherine's house, though better authenticated than John Knox's, has suffered at the hands of a more ceremonious and reconstructive brand of piety. All the rooms have been converted into chapels, from which her disturbing spirit has been banished by a well-meant clutter of bondieuseries, dusty disconnected relics, and sixteenth-century or later frescoes of her life by third-rate artists. Nor, for the profane, is the loggia wrongly ascribed to Peruzzi worth the visit. It is better to go up the hill to San Domenico and look at Andrea Vanni's portrait of her. She was only thirty-three when she died; this likeness suggests that she was much older. The Sienese eyes have lost their felinity and become the slits of an introvert or of a sick woman. But there can be no doubt that this picture gives a better idea of what she looked like either than Sodoma's sugary though well-composed fresco on the left side of the altar in her chapel there, which shows her receiving the stigmata,* or than the much prized relic of her head which may also be seen and which, exposed to view in a glass box, is unpleasantly paraded through the streets on 30 April. [*Plate* 34.]

Her age, more prolific of disturbances than of art, nevertheless added its bit to the cathedral. After Lando di Pietro's great unpractical arches had been abandoned, work

* The rival Franciscan order objected that this miracle infringed some sort of supernatural copyright in their founder's favour, one which St. Francis himself would have been the last person to claim. Successive popes, prodded this way and that, made conflicting pronouncements. The subject may be left to those who think they can reconcile these dicta.

was resumed on the old Duomo. By 1370 the choir above the baptistery was completed, though the east end was never finished off outside. As much as there is, is good; it is the work of Jacopo di Mino del Pellicciaio. The choir stalls with their remarkable inlaid work by Francesco del Tonghio also date from this time, all except the central ones in the apse which were added two hundred years later.

Of the same period (about 1370) are the first sections of the vast marble pavement which, in the course of the next hundred and ninety years, was extended over the whole floor of the cathedral. A score of leading artists worked on it at various dates and in various styles. Probably the first design of all (though what we see, as in some other cases, is a modern copy) is the heraldic panel; the second, going up the nave, and the only one in mosaic—it represents the Wolf of Siena surrounded by the symbolic beasts of allied cities. All the others are of inlaid marble with graffiti. Two other panels in the nave and the five virtues in the choir are fourteenth-century; the rest is Renaissance work. Modern taste prefers the earlier graffiti in simple outline, as more suitable for a pavement, to the later complicated three-dimensional renderings with graduated shading. These reach their climax in the hexagonal section under the dome and in the panels immediately east of it, which were done by Beccafumi in the sixteenth century. Altogether, the pavement is something unique, and when exposed greatly enhances the view up the nave. Unfortunately some of the best parts are usually preserved beneath wooden floorboards, except from mid-August to mid-September. English tourists have been complaining about this unavailingly since 1658.*

For any disappointment on this account the visitor in search of fresh sensations is amply compensated by the western façade as completed in 1377 by Giovanni di Cecco and others, after Giovanni Pisano's restraining influence had been forgotten.† This great screen, which fraudulently suggests that the nave and aisle roofs are much higher than they really are, is one of the most splendidly undisciplined things in Italy, all dazzling white Carrara marble and mosaics, the not very convincing lines of its architecture happily blurred by a multitude of sculptures in the round which surge outwards from every foothold. Can this be the art of the victorious social revolution, a late medieval equivalent of the Stalinesque? Presumably the *Riformatori* had the decisive word in choosing it. Southbound travellers should compare it with the superficially similar but better designed and more restrained façade at Orvieto, which is probably a little earlier. Certainly Orvieto's rose-window, with its delicate tracery and the square of well-proportioned sculpture round it, is pleasanter than the abrupt, glum hole at Siena, which looks like a vortex in the froth. But there is something to be said for the Siena front, all the same. Orvieto's is chilly. Should a wedding-cake be chaste, or exuberant? [*Plate* 33.]

Both of these west fronts, incidentally, should be seen at night, when Siena's in particular gains considerably from floodlighting or plain moonlight, and one is more inclined to accept Sir Thomas Hoby's opinion that 'it may be reckoned emong the

* See *Francis Mortoft, his Book* (Hakluyt Society). A detailed account of the pavement will be found in R. H. H. Cust, *The Pavement Masters of Siena* (Bell, 1901).

† The latter's work on the lower half of the façade was described on page 57.

sumptious woorkes of Europe', and even almost to agree with Evelyn's verdict that it is 'of inexpressible beauty'.

Presumably Ruskin saw it without this advantage. 'I had a bad weary headache at Siena,' he wrote, 'and the cathedral seemed to me every way absurd—over-cut, over-striped, over-crocketed, over-gabled, a piece of costly confectionery, and faithless vanity.'

Less disturbed by its faithlessness, but even more pained by its neglect of Vitruvius, was Addison in 1701:

> 'There is nothing in this city so extraordinary as the cathedral, which a man may view with pleasure after he has seen St. Peter's, though it is quite of another make, and can only be looked upon as one of the master-pieces of *Gothic* architecture. When a man sees the prodigious pains and expence that our forefathers have been at in these barbarous buildings, one cannot but fancy to himself what miracles of architecture they would have left us, had they only been instructed in the right way. . . .
>
> 'The very spouts are loaden with ornaments; the windows are formed like so many scenes of perspective, with a multitude of little pillars retiring one behind another; the great columns are finely engraven with fruits and foliage that run twisting about them from the very top to the bottom; the whole body of the church is chequered with different lays of white and black marble, the pavement curiously cut out in designs and scripture-stories, and the font covered with such a variety of figures, and over-run with so many little mazes and labyrinths of sculpture, that nothing in the world can make a prettier shew to those, who prefer false beauties, and affected ornaments, to a noble and majestic simplicity.'*

The visitor is now invited to pronounce his own judgement on this most Italian of cathedrals. Is it too much to hope that it may be tempered by affection for the warm-hearted character of the people who built it?

* Joseph Addison, *Remarks on several parts of Italy.*

7

Renaissance Siena as it was

AFTER THE FALL of the *Riformatori*, the Sienese were apparently played out. In the course of about two centuries the commune had fairly run the gamut of possible régimes from right to left. It had been proved that no party or class could rule alone and permanently mould the state to serve its interests. Henceforth there were coalitions. Their permutations need not detain us. The parties or *monti* gradually ceased to represent social forces and declined into caucuses of politicians. A fifth, the *monte del popolo*, came into being, but it represented little more than its sponsors' ingenuity in filching a historic name.

With the decline of Sienese industry and commerce, landowning became once more the principal source of wealth. All who could, small shopkeepers as well as big bankers, invested in agriculture, and in many cases found their farms more profitable than their businesses. They stayed on in Siena, of course, for a house in town brought full citizenship and a civilized life. But purely urban economic issues and the class struggles of guildsmen and financiers were less important than they had been. The *monti* or parties, though still mainly hereditary, ceased to be more than a blurred reflection of class interests. Some aristocratic families had been admitted as members of the popular parties during the turmoils of the mid-fourteenth century (the Chigi and the Spannocchi, both leading bankers, are examples), while others, though still belonging to upper-crust *monti*, had sunk economically and now followed modest trades. Two large groups remained second-class citizens; they were the farm workers and the bulk of those who had moved into the town to fill the gap left by the Black Death. On these lines Sienese society, following the economy, began to ossify, a slow and not uncomfortable process.

Was the age of the city-state over? It looked like it. Florence had swallowed up Arezzo and had snatched away Cortona and Montepulciano from the Sienese. War with Florence broke out for the first time in a hundred and twenty years. Beyond the Apennines Giangaleazzo Visconti, duke of Milan, was extending his conquests and pressed in a wide arc upon the northern frontiers of Florence. His ambitions and prospects were great. Siena joined in alliance with him and in 1399, exhausted by war and internal misfortunes, placed itself under his sovereignty. Pisa had already done so. The duke, an enlightened man, allowed local self-government. For a moment the time seemed ripe for wider loyalties. If Giangaleazzo had succeeded in making himself king of Italy, as he planned to do as soon as Florence had fallen, the nation might well have achieved unity several centuries earlier.

Instead, he suddenly died, and in a year or two Siena, like some other parts of his dominions, recovered its independence. The city-state was reprieved for another century and a half.

Perhaps that is too negative a way of putting it. Our view of the Italian communes has been unduly influenced by the Florentine historians, who have distorted anything tending to show that their city was not the most democratic of all. In fact, the social upheaval of the *Ciompi* in 1378 was almost the last kick of democracy in Florence, after which that city slumbered politically under the clever rule of merchant oligarchs and then of the Medici, with only two brief awakenings. Meanwhile in Siena it was dictatorships that were short-lived and popular coalitions that were the rule. Not one of these later constitutional experiments was altogether a success, but the effort to maintain a free society was inexhaustible, and deserves more sympathy than it usually gets.

The winter of 1423–1424 saw Siena briefly involved in issues bigger than those of communal politics. The conciliar movement stood at the height of its prestige. It was a most well-meant attempt to reform the Church by setting representative institutions in the place of papal autocracy. The Council of Constance, wielding unexpected authority, had at last succeeded in getting rid of three simultaneous popes and thus in ending the schism that had defied St. Catherine's more partisan interventions. By decreeing further councils at regular intervals, not subject to papal veto, it had laid foundations for more reforms and for the practical supremacy of councils over popes. Unfortunately the pope himself had other ideas. Martin V had the temper of a Renaissance despot rather than that of a modern prime minister. H. A. L. Fisher says of him that he placed the papacy before the Church, Italy before Europe, and his Colonna kinsmen before everybody. Although he could not prevent the next council from meeting, he had it moved from Pavia to Siena and worked assiduously for its failure. First he tried delaying tactics—he promised to attend in person, but did not. Then he infiltrated into the gathering various clerics from Rome who had no right to attend, tried to confine business to such safe matters as repeating the condemnation of Wyclif and Hus, and inspired some quiet sabotage by the presiding prelate. By these methods the Council of Siena was reduced to a state of torpor and despair which has not been unknown in more recent international conferences. Seeing the rot setting in, the Sienese closed their city gates to keep the delegates from leaving (the council had been good for trade), but before two dangerous proposals could be debated the papal legates escaped from the town and, once safely over the Florentine border, proclaimed the council dissolved. One is glad to record that the last stand against all this chicanery was made by the abbot of Paisley, but, inexcusably, the few remaining delegates would not stay even to hear Latin fulminations delivered in the accents of Glasgow.

This period of Sienese history is interesting not for its politics but for its personalities.

Indeed for some fifty years after the death of Giangaleazzo the political calm lasted so uncannily long that presently the bored young men of the town formed two rival gangs of fifteenth-century teddy-boys, 'Shindy' and 'Scratch', which engaged in non-political street-fighting just for the hell of it. The *balìa*, the new inner commission who from now on ran Siena, had to deal with them sternly.

A country-born Sienese who literally left his mark on his city at this time was San Bernardino. A wandering Franciscan preacher of the Strict Observance, sincere and effective (unlike Boccaccio's friars), he was nowhere more popular than in his native city. Sano di Pietro's pictures, painted at the time, show him addressing kneeling crowds in the Campo or in front of the Franciscan church, with a canvas partition coyly dividing the sexes. A personal friend of some of the early humanists, he avoided their pretentious style and in racy sermons, spiced with good stories and local slang, denounced the vices and vendettas of his fellow-citizens. He was particularly down on cosmetics which, as manufactured by the apothecaries of the period, apparently smelled most peculiar and harmed the skin; but feminine mentality being what it is, few of his lady penitents heeded his repeated warnings against a 'stink of sulphur' that might prove everlasting. He had more success in his campaign against gambling. When a dice-maker pointed out that this was ruining his trade, the saint with great presence of mind told him to make plaques instead, having the letters *I.H.S.* within the sun's rays. He took this symbol into the pulpit with him and soon, in that sunlit country which prefers a gesture to a reformation, plaques of this kind were prominently affixed to the façades of the Palazzo Pubblico, the gates and other buildings, where they can be seen to this day. [*Plate* 32.]

Among the shoals of saints in the Art Gallery, San Bernardino's features catch the eye. Once seen, his round head, long nose, down-turned mouth, and very pointed chin are never forgotten. Pandering to the shallow piety of their patrons, some artists have given the doubtless ascetic face of this lively and observant man an expression which we today can only describe as moonstruck. He deserved better. [*Plate* 36.]

In one of those crowds listening to San Bernardino on the Campo was a bright young man of the kind with which the central streets of Italian cities always seem to shimmer. The son of an impoverished country gentleman, in his third year at the university, a promising writer of verse, carefully dressed beyond his means, precocious, hard-working but very fond of the good things of life, including women. Such young Italians often belie their agate exterior and this one was genuinely touched by San Bernardino's message. 'I was so carried away by him,' he wrote long afterwards, 'that I very nearly entered his order.' Very nearly, but not quite. The Middle Ages had gone and Renaissance Man, no longer single-minded, was there, even in Siena.

Æneas Sylvius Piccolomini, instead of joining the Franciscans, stayed in a world that was made for young men like him. He went about, he worked late hours at law, he scribbled hexameters in his spare time. He wrote more than two thousand lines of Latin verse, the *Nymphiplexis*, on a Sienese friend's entanglement with his mistress. He recorded the goings-on when the emperor Sigismund III came on his way to Rome, and all the young ladies of Siena took in the qualities of his courtiers through the corners of their little cats' eyes. Afterwards he wrote a best-selling novel about this visit, *De Duobus Amantibus* or *Euryalus and Lucretia*, which a more strait-laced age has castigated as 'most unedifying' and which he himself in his more respectable years never quite lived down, despite his disingenuous complaint that people read the indelicate story and ignored the moral.

Finding Siena too small for him, Æneas joined the suite of a dissident cardinal who was passing through on his way to the Council of Basel, where reforming churchmen hoped to avenge the Council of Siena's failure. From this point on Pinturicchio's series of ten paintings in the cathedral library are the best introduction to his life. The only important thing they conceal is that at Basel (whither we see him bound, rather self-conscious on a white stallion) he was deeply involved with the extreme wing of the conciliar movement, writing its propaganda, plotting to kidnap the pope and on intimate terms with the antipope Felix V, whose secretary he became. [*Plate* 42.]

Before he got that far he was sent on a diplomatic mission to Edinburgh, in Italian eyes today still something of an Ultima Thule, and in 1435 much more so. The object was to induce James I of Scotland to threaten the border and so prevent the English from renewing the Hundred Years' War. It was winter. A gale drove his ship to the coast of Norway. On reaching Scotland he was nearly wrecked off Dunbar and, while fulfilling a vow to go barefoot to the church at Whitekirk, he contracted rheumatism or gout in the feet which lasted the rest of his life. The mission was a failure. The ship which was to have taken him back, and in which he wisely refused to embark, sank with all hands just outside harbour, and he had to travel through England in disguise. In his *Commentaries* he has left an account of the Northern Kingdom which need not wound Scottish feelings if we make some allowance for the bias induced by his bad luck with the weather.

> 'A cold land, but indifferently fertile, and much of it bare of trees. Beneath the soil a sulphureous stone is found which they dig out and burn for fuel. The towns lack walls and the houses are built for the most part without lime; the farms are roofed with turfs and in the country an ox-hide serves to close the door. The common people are poor and uncouth; they eat meat and fish in abundance, but bread as a delicacy. The men are short of stature and bold, the women fair and graceful and disposed to venery. To kiss a woman is of less account among them than to shake hands in Italy. They have no wine, save what is imported. . . . There is nothing the Scots hear more gladly than disparagement of the English. They say that Scotland is composed of two parts, the one cultivated, the other wild and almost without husbandry. The wild Scots speak another language and at times have only the bark of trees for food. No wolves are found in Scotland and the crow is rare, and for that reason the tree in which it builds its nest is forfeit to the royal exchequer. At the time of the winter solstice (and that was when I was there) the day does not last for more than four hours in Scotland. . . . For this country of Scotland and the parts of England adjoining it have nothing to compare with our habitations, being but an untamed wilderness untouched by the winter sun.'*

* *Commentarii Pii Papae Secundi*, pp. 4–5.

'—*Horrida, inculta, atque hiemali sole inaccessa.*' One can see poor Æneas Sylvius, back safely on the Continent, dictating the words to his secretary as he rubs his chilblains. Had he never seen coal before? How did he come to misunderstand about the wolves and half understand about the crows? *Apart from what he saw for himself, his impressions of Scotland must have been powerful but hazy, like those the modern traveller gathers from the obscure outpourings of his hosts in a Balkan railway carriage. And were even his own observations always quite accurate?

On returning to the Rhineland from his Scottish jaunt, he resumed his anti-Roman activities and also turned his hand to poetry, history, and a Who's Who, writing learnedly on the care of horses and the miseries of courtiers. When the Council of Basel was discredited, he became secretary to the new emperor Frederick III, who greatly admired his literary work and crowned him poet laureate. Then, visiting Rome as Frederick's envoy to the pope, he was converted both opportunely and sincerely, after the fashion of the time, to the church's cause. He resolved 'to abandon Venus for Bacchus' and, more important still, repudiated all allegiance to the remnants of the conciliar movement. He met the right cardinals. He had the right contacts abroad. He was just the man to send on a delicate mission to bribe the archbishop of Mainz. He entered the priesthood, became papal secretary, then bishop of Trieste, then bishop of his native town.

At Siena he had an anxious moment introducing the emperor to his hitherto unseen bride, a Portuguese princess. To everybody's great relief, she was pretty, and a charming little Renaissance column marks the spot where they met, five hundred yards beyond the Porta Camollia. This column appears too in Pinturicchio's fresco, but alas! his delicious landscape is no more, and the column rises forlornly from a suburban pavement. [*Plate* 43.]

When the Turks took Constantinople, Æneas befriended the Greek scholars and prelates who came westwards, bringing classical texts and possibilities of reunion with the Orthodox church. He made the fate of the Byzantines his favourite cause. It seemed an important one at that moment, and he received a cardinal's hat. Of course the success-story could have only one ending, and two years later they made him pope, to avoid having to elect a Frenchman. With hard work, freedom from inconvenient loyalties, and a good Latin style, a diplomat could go far in the Renaissance. For such a lover of Virgil, no other name than Pius was thinkable.

Siena was delighted. A pope could be expected to do much for his native city. Above all his political protection would be welcome. *Condottieri* were still a nuisance. There had been that trouble with a treacherous and financially importunate general employed by the Sienese government; he became so impossible that they lured him away from his soldiery and threw him out of the council-chamber window, a much admired stratagem which started something of a craze for defenestration in municipal circles. To make quite sure of the new pope's benevolence, the city fathers admitted his kinsfolk to full civic rights—the Piccolomini, as *grandi*, had been excluded since 1277. But to their

* It was the other way round; a recent law which forbade 'the bigging of ruikis in treis' had made these birds scarcer.

dismay Pius II held out for equal rights for all the *grandi* and when he eventually got that, even pleaded for the much misliked *dodicini* too. That they refused him and he had to be content. Then, after this mutually gratifying piece of hard bargaining, came the pontiff's triumphal visit to his *dulcissima patria* and the shower of favours—the see of Siena raised to an archbishopric, the Golden Rose for the city, and the right arm of John the Baptist for the cathedral, St. Catherine canonized at last. Pius himself built a loggia and his relations palaces—mostly by fashionable architects from Florence. Hostile aggression was ruled out and the economy boomed. It was a long time since Siena had had it so good.

Pius II was a worthy but hardly a great pope. For that he was a little too much of an opportunist, and anyway he was only there for six years. His plea to those who were so tactless as to quote from his youthful writings—'Reject Æneas, accept Pius!'—was not universally complied with, even in that easy-going age. Though he was now at last desperately in earnest about a cause, that of the crusade, his conference with the powers at Mantua failed to help the Greeks, and he is chiefly remembered by church historians for the Bull *Execrabilis*, a fulmination in the direst terms which this erstwhile supporter of the conciliar movement launched against any who should appeal from a pope's authority to a Council's. Yet he had the charm, if not the consistency, of a scholar. A compulsive writer, he put down everything on paper, and emerges from these self-revelations as *molto simpatico*. In spite of the rheumatism contracted at Dunbar, his favourite recreation was to picnic in the countryside, to the dismay of his town-bred cardinals. His views on morals were more enlightened than those of many ecclesiastics then or later. 'I know human nature,' he wrote. 'Whoever does not have affairs in youth has them in old age, and makes himself ridiculous. I know too how love kindles unsuspected virtues. As bees gather honey from flowers, so should you gather goodness from your love-affairs.' He disappointed those men of letters who had expected much from his patronage; he said he would rather exchange verses than buy them. Possibly his best aphorism was, '*Dignitatibus viros dandos, non dignitates hominibus*'—'Finding men fit for honours, not honours for men.' [*Plate* 35.]

He died in 1464 at the seaport of Ancona, waiting for ships and men to assemble for the crusade on which he had set his heart. Glad of the excuse, it never sailed. After all, why should it?

Turkish wars were at the back of people's minds in Siena just then—unpleasant Asiatic swordsmen perpetrate the *Massacres of the Innocents* depicted by Matteo di Giovanni in three Sienese churches. All the more reason for enjoying life while it lasted. An excerpt from Allegretto's *Diari*, nicely translated by Edmund Gardner,* gives a glimpse of a *festa* in the summer of 1463, when the duchess of Calabria was entertained.

> 'In honour of the said Duchess, there was arranged by the Arts a most beauteous pageant and dance at the foot of the Palace of the Signori, and there were invited as many worthy young women and girls as Siena had, who came right well adorned with robes and jewels, and young men to dance. And there was made a great she-wolf, all gilded,

* *Story of Siena*, p. 129.

out of which came a morris-dance of twelve persons, right well and richly adorned, and one dressed like a nun, and they danced to a canzone that begins; "She won't be a nun any more." And at the said dance a goodly collation was provided of marchpanes and other cakes in abundance, with fruit of every kind according to the season. To the said Duchess and her nobles it seemed a fair thing and a rich pageant, and that she-wolf pleased them immensely, and they thought that we had lovely women.'

Sixteen years later the Sienese enjoyed a brief triumph when they helped to beat a Florentine army once again at Poggio Imperiale near Poggibonsi. Then, bored to distraction with their last golden age, they started the biggest and longest *trafuglío* in their history. This is the period of which de Commynes was thinking when he wrote that Siena '*est de tout temps en partialité, et se gouverne plus follement que ville d'Italie*'. Only the most resolute of historians can hack a path through the tangle of changing factions, family vendettas, conspiracies of nobles, popular uprisings, foreign interventions, restorations, liberations, perpetual banishments, and solemn reconciliations. One hopes and suspects that the Sienese took these happenings more lightheartedly than we would. At the height of the performance four of the most ponderous burghers of the *noveschi*, together with a plebeian for good measure, were simultaneously defenestrated from the Palazzo.

The solemn reconciliations were evidently masterpieces of Latin ceremonial. Here is a contemporary description of one of them, staged in the Duomo on New Year's Eve, 1494, a fit counterpart to the *festa* described above by the same writer.

'The conditions of the peace were then read, which took up eight pages, together with an oath of the most horrible sort, full of maledictions, imprecations, excommunications, invocations of evil, renunciation of benefits temporal and spiritual, confiscation of goods, vows, and so many other woes that to hear it was a terror; they even swore that on the death-bed no sacrament should accrue to the salvation, but rather to the damnation of those who might break the said conditions; insomuch that I, Allegretto di Nanni Allegretti, being present, believe that never was made or heard a more awful and horrible oath. Then the notaries of the *Nove* and the *Popolo*, on either side of the altar, wrote down the names of all the citizens, who swore upon the crucifix, for on each side there was one, and every couple of the one and the other faction kissed; and the bells clashed, and *Te Deum laudamus* was sung with the organs and the choir while the oath was being taken. All this happened between one and two hours of the night, with many torches lighted. Now may God will that this be peace indeed, and tranquillity for all citizens, whereof I doubt.'*

Allegretto knew his Siena. A scene like this had but the briefest effect on what is sometimes claimed to have been the most religious-minded population in Italy. The disturbances continued, off and on, for about twenty years. But at half-time some sort of

* Allegretto, *Diari Senesi*, pp. 836–837, as translated by J. A. Symonds in his *Renaissance in Italy—The Age of the Despots*, p. 558.

breathing-space was provided for the poor diarist and his like, though not quite in the form he hoped for, by the personal rule of Pandolfo Petrucci, or rather by its more effective periods. Pandolfo's government, though interrupted, lasted from 1497 to 1512. This sharp-eyed dictator derived his power from wealth, display, a canny foreign policy, sixty assassinations, considerable popularity with all classes, and in the first place, as his admirer Machiavelli noted, from command of the city guard. His secretary, when asked by that other connoisseur of despotism, Pope Alexander VI, how the volatile Sienese were held down, answered briefly, 'With lies, Holy Father.' Pandolfo lived in considerable state; he had the sumptuary laws of Siena waived for his womenfolk and never walked through the streets without a cortège of servile patricians. But he was clever enough to be content with informal authority and his choice of the title of *Magnifico* was considered, in that age of resounding lordships, as an attractive mark of modesty.

This relatively unassuming autocracy resembles that of Cosimo dei Medici and might, like his, have become dynastic, if the Sienese had been as tame as the Florentines and Pandolfo's successors less degenerate than they were. After his death power passed in quick succession through the hands of four other Petrucci—the spoilt Borghese, who dismissed his father's wily secretary, was expelled and went mad; the violent Cardinal Raffaello, who died unexpectedly in such a thunderstorm that men thought the mouth of hell had opened for him; the brutal Francesco, whom Clement VII enticed to Rome and locked up; and Fabio, too handsome and too amorous, who was thrown out to the overdue slogan of '*Popolo e Libertà!*'

But the tide of tyranny was coming in with a gale behind it. Siena was now a target for foreign military adventurers on a bigger scale. Already the duke of Calabria, eldest son of the king of Naples, who had helped to win the victory of Poggio Imperiale over Florence in 1479, had hung round afterwards plotting to add Siena to his dominions. And in 1503 none other than Cesare Borgia came spurring over the clay uplands towards Siena, 'to make of that city a state to his own liking', which meant the temporary departure of that other blackguard, Pandolfo Petrucci. A small community whose means of defence had become blunted could only survive with difficulty in the jungle of Central Italian power-politics, in which the beasts of prey were becoming bigger every year, and on either of these two occasions Siena would have been swallowed up at a gulp but for the good fortune that both of these carnivores were suddenly interrupted by others.

More surprisingly, in 1524, just after the expulsion of Fabio Petrucci, the regent of Scotland arrived on the scene. Like everyone else, he too began to tinker with the Sienese constitution. John Stewart, duke of Albany, had recently left the thankless task of trying to steer Scottish policy in a pro-French direction after Flodden and had returned to the service of his adopted country, France. Passing through the town with a large French force, he dashed the hopes of the republican party, the *libertini*, by helping to set up a dictatorship of big merchants. A man who was wont to throw his bonnet in the fire when crossed was not to be trifled with, so long as he was there, but after he had gone the *libertini* overthrew the merchants. The latter had powerful friends abroad, and the year 1526 saw the guns of the Medici pope and his Florentine allies pounding at the Porta Camollia. The Sienese, with some of their old Ghibelline spirit, remembered Montaperti, rededicated their city to the Virgin and in a sudden sortie miraculously routed the far more numerous Medicean troops, who fled for ten miles with their general, a warrior renowned for his corpulence, puffing half-dressed at their head.

The Habsburg empire, fresh from a more important victory at Pavia, was now spreading its sombre control over central Italy. Siena accepted Charles V's protection and a Spanish garrison. Its unpopularity was noted by one of the first English tourists, Sir Thomas Hoby of Bisham Abbey in Berkshire, who spent some months here in 1549–1550. He observes of the Spanish commander, Don Diego de Mendoza, that 'at his cumming he was alwaies more honorablie receaved outwardlie then inwardlie beloved'. Perhaps feeling his social isolation, Don Diego asked Hoby to dine with him and extended the invitation to all the other Englishmen then in Siena, of whom there were no less than nine, quite a colony. Hoby thinks that the foreign occupation 'appearethe cheeflie to proceade of their private discention and intestine discorde in that they cann not be brought to anie agreement betwext them selves. For they are divided into fowre severall partes . . .'—of which parties he gives an understandably confused history, though he notes the basic fact of Sienese politics that, whatever régime was in power, from time to time the people 'cloyed with this kind of government' and 'repined greatlie' against it. He says that 'most of the handsommest gentlmen in the citie' belong to the *noveschi*, who have hitherto been the pro-Spanish party.*

But when Don Diego started to build a fortress on the north-western edge of the city, obviously designed to dominate rather than to protect, it was 'full sore against their willes'. The work went ponderously ahead in the Spanish manner, despite direct appeals to Charles V, renewed public prayers to the Madonna and the unnerving presence of a half-mad hermit, who appropriately howled the 127th psalm while brandishing a crucifix and a skull, and presently took to throwing stones at the foreman.†

At last, when the formidable Don Diego was absent, the Sienese rose. One Æneas Piccolomini, a great-grand-nephew of Pius II, had secretly collected a small force in the *contado*, together with some French allies. Entering by the southern gates, he drove the Spaniards into their fortress on the site of the present Fortezza. There they capitulated. For this, Hoby tells us, 'Don Diego was blamed and somwhat in displeasure with th' Emperor.' As the Spaniards marched out with the honours of war, their commander congratulated the Sienese on their exploit, but added that they should be careful in future, for they had offended too great a man.

* *A Booke of the Travaile and Lief of me, Thomas Hoby, with diverse things woorth the notinge* (Camden Misc. X, ed. E. Powell, 1902).

† For their fortress the Spaniards used stones from the ancient fortified towers of the patricians, many of which they began to demolish at the same time. The fortress was demolished in its turn after the Spaniards had gone, and the *Tavolette* of 1551 and 1552 show the citizens happily at work on this task.

8

Renaissance Siena as it is

IT WAS THE sculptor Jacopo della Quercia who brought in the Renaissance. His two chief creations here were the first Sienese works which, though still transitional, definitely broke away from the belated medievalism that clung so tenaciously to these hilltops. What better vehicle for a new style than a fountain? Unfortunately, his Fonte Gaia in the Campo, finished in 1419, has received so many hard knocks from centuries of carelessness and Palios that its remnants have had to be taken to the top floor of the Palazzo Pubblico for better preservation, while a modern copy now stands on the original site at the top of the concave piazza.

His other work, the font in the baptistery below the cathedral choir, dates from about ten years later. It owes its graceful form and some of its detail to him, but all the lower figures and five of the bronze reliefs on the hexagon are by others, including Ghiberti and Donatello. These reliefs are very well known, for every book on early Renaissance sculpture reproduces them, in order to compare the differences in style and the varying progress made just at this time by the different artists in rendering spatial depth. The late Gothic baptistery itself is rather dingy and disappointing, but the font lifts it out of the ordinary.

Another work of the early *quattrocento*, transitional in a more pedestrian way, is the Loggia della Mercanzía, built at the central crossroads as a meeting-place for the merchants' guilds and their tribunal. As befits a commercial building, its effect is more solid and sumptuous than graceful. Once again the decorative details are the work of various sculptors. Vecchietta's emaciated statues make an amusing contrast with Federighi's well-fed ones, and the left-hand marble bench by Urbano da Cortona is an improvement on the right-hand one by Federighi. The piers and the canopies over the saints outside are still semi-Gothic, and the building as a whole lacks distinction, comparing unfavourably with loggias in other cities. The storey above was added much later and improves it.

At this time the enlightened Signory had established a town-planning commission with considerable powers, *Gli Ufficiali sopra l'Ornato della Città*. Such bodies, however, concern themselves more with maintaining existing standards and preventing eyesores than with promoting architectural progress, and Siena might have gone on for some time longer with rather half-hearted attempts at the new style, or have returned to brick Gothic as in the Buonsignori palace, built as late as the 1450s, but for the impulse given by Pius II. His decade and the next one saw a remarkable flowering of civil architecture in the town, commissioned in almost all cases by members of the Piccolomini clan and others closely connected with His Holiness. The financial basis for all this construction was, surprisingly, not so much papal nepotism as municipal tax concessions for buildings of merit. Moreover, this new adornment of the city was strongly Florentine in inspiration. Provincialism, a defect from which Renaissance art can least of all afford to suffer, was at last effectively banished.

In 1462 Pius himself built the Loggia del Papa, as its inscription tells us, 'for his kinsmen the Piccolomini'. It is Federighi's masterpiece, and its proportions are a great improvement on the older loggia's. Pius' cousins the Turchi employed the same architect to refurbish the quaint brick mansion known as the Palazzo dei Diavoli, half a mile or so beyond the northern gate. The pope's sister built the Palazzo delle Papesse (now the Banca d'Italia) and his nephews the Palazzo Piccolomini. These two palaces were designed by the Florentine Bernardo Rossellino and executed by Federighi and Porrina respectively. The Palazzo Piccolomini, which now houses the city archives, is unquestionably the best building of the period in Siena. The material is good sound travertine, the lines are beautifully restrained, the proportions perfect. High above the entrance are the Piccolomini arms, whose lunettes of heraldic half-moons have been cleverly and sparingly used as a decorative motif below the cornice and above the windows, while the elegant wrought-iron tethering rings along the base of the façade have also been given that shape. It is quite as good as anything in Florence. [*Plate* 39].

The relation to the Florentine prototypes is interesting. Rossellino had previously built the Rucellai palace there to Alberti's designs, which introduced pilasters running up the walls and heavy intermediate cornices between the storeys. But when he came to build his palaces in Siena, Rossellino preferred to leave these out and go back to the classic simplicity of Michelozzo's Palazzo Medici-Riccardi, the original model for all Florentine Renaissance palaces, or more exactly to its first floor. The Palazzo Piccolomini windows, however, were taken from those of the Rucellai.

Another Florentine architect, Giuliano da Maiano, built the Palazzo Spannocchi in the Via Banchi di Sopra for the pope's treasurer. If architectural display is any guide, the latter worthy knew his job better than did the poet Cecco's grandfather some two centuries earlier. But of course the perquisites had increased. In fact the prevailing weakness of popes in their dealings with the Sienese seems to have been not nepotism, but accountancy. This palace also resembles the Medici-Riccardi one in Florence, except that it too lacks the disproportionately heavy rustication of the ground-floor masonry, comforting though this might have been to the owners at moments of political stress. And it has what is perhaps an even finer cornice, with a row of bull-necked Roman emperors' heads below it. It is a magnificent building, but a little lifeless, perhaps because of restoration. Giuliano da Maiano also built a less imposing town house in the south-eastern quarter for the abbot of San Galgano, having rosettes instead of roundels above the windows and an extra string-course running across them, spoiling the design. Today it is sadly dilapidated. Both of Giuliano's palaces are built of yellow *tufo*, whereas Rossellino's are of fine grey travertine. In fact Rossellino comes out better in all respects.

All Sienese palaces, whether Renaissance like the Piccolomini or Gothic like the nearby Sansedoni, have the same fortress-like ground floors designed to keep out assassins and rioters. They were less adapted to resist the onslaughts of James Boswell when he came here in the summer of 1765.* His visit is worth a brief digression. Having made the unoriginal discovery that 'the Florentines (especially the Florentine women) are very proud and very mercenary', he had moved to Siena, where he was completely enchanted with the aristocracy's freedom of manners. Here he spent a delightful month reading 'the divine Ariosto' every day, learning Italian and the flute, and having purposeful affairs with two married ladies simultaneously. In telling Rousseau of these last activities in a long letter, he would have him believe that he only yielded broadmindedly to local custom. 'The times, Sir, are much changed in Italy. No longer does one have to fear the stiletto of a jealous husband.' Signora Porzia Sansedoni allowed no more than a flirtation, despite one of Boswell's postscripts which said, 'P.P.S. Read this letter with care. It contains very, very romantic sentiments.' But Signora Girólama Piccolomini was a simpler soul. 'This amiable person, whose heart was already touched, listened to me kindly and granted me all, saying, "*Ebbene, mi fido a voi come a un galantuomo.*" ' And she was disconsolate after he had gone back home to Scotland.

Boswell's reaction to all this was entirely Boswellian, just as the reply of the good Sienese priest in whom he confided was a perfect example of the over-optimistic politeness of Italy.

> 'I am now in a beautiful town in Tuscany,' he writes. 'I am well thought of by all the nobility. I enjoy the honest friendship of some pleasant ladies. I am studying the beautiful Italian language and making good progress. I am also studying music with an excellent teacher; I play my flute and sing with real enjoyment. I am enjoying good health. The weather is clear and agreeable. I can do everything I wish. I am in a situation which I imagined in my most delicious moments. And yet I cannot say I am happy. I am surprised at this. I don't know what to think. I don't know what to look for. Undoubtedly, in this world no man can be completely happy. Oh, no—sad thought! Abbé Crocchi, my esteemed instructor, advises me to consider this lack of happiness as a strong proof of the immortality of the soul, and of a better life in another world.'

Those whose temperament calls for a more bracing theology than this, wherever it may lead to, may care to glance at a tablet less than two hundred yards down the street from Girolama Piccolomini's palace. It marks the house of Lelio and Fausto Sozzini, the sixteenth-century founders of Socinianism and principal forerunners of the modern Unitarians. Fausto was descended on his mother's side from Pandolfo Petrucci. They

* See *Boswell on the Grand Tour—Italy, Corsica and France*, Yale edition (Heinemann, 1955).

had to emigrate to Switzerland and Poland to develop their ideas, for Siena, after Duke Cosimo had taken over, was not propitious to anything but the most abject orthodoxy. Another Sienese reformer, Bernardo Ochino, was invited to England by Cranmer, expelled swiftly again by Mary, and finished up in eastern Europe too. Early Sienese visitors to our islands seem to have been uniformly uncomfortable there.

The churches of this period, unlike the palaces, are mostly the work of Sienese architects, though some outside influence is apparent. The most impressive are the large nave of the Servi, designed by the leading Sienese architect of the day, Baldassare Peruzzi, and the Hospital church with a good coffered ceiling, decorative galleries for choir and organ, and a statue by Vecchietta above the altar. The smaller Renaissance interiors such as San Sebastiano in Valle Piatta, the Fontegiusta, and Santa Maria delle Nevi are not always easy of access. The last-named one, by Francesco di Giorgio, is worth trying, as it contains Matteo di Giovanni's best picture.

The Sienese school of painting died with Neroccio.* The next generation, it is true, produced Beccafumi and Sodoma, who were Sienese by birth and adoption respectively, but there is nothing distinctively Sienese in their painting. We have seen Sodoma, whose family name was Bazzi, in the St. Catherine frescoes in San Domenico and will see him again at the monastery of Monte Oliveto. There are many pictures of his scattered about the town, notably in the Oratory of San Bernardino. His work is clever, showy, and not overburdened with sincerity, though here and there a figure or a group stands out. Beccafumi, a local peasant boy by origin, was one of the first Mannerists. In dimly lit chapels one comes across his alarming altarpieces, all clouds and contortions, mercifully hidden under many layers of varnish. The next change of fashion in Italian art will quite likely make Mannerism the rage, so aspiring art-snobs should store the rather aptly named Beccafumi in their armoury. With luck, the craze will be short-lived.

In the field of sculpture, Jacopo della Quercia was followed by Vecchietta who, it will be remembered, was a painter as well, in which medium his saintly greybeards and 'tottering frames' have been a target for the more robust. His best-known piece of bronze is the tabernacle over the high altar in the Duomo. More in keeping with his pictures are the two outer statues on the Loggia della Mercanzía. In a much higher class is Lorenzo di Mariano, or Marrina, a Sienese Renaissance sculptor who deserves to be better known. Everyone sees (and too often passes without examining) his carved doorways leading out of the cathedral into the library and into the circular chapel which contains Donatello's fine bronze statue of John the Baptist, well set against the intricate dull gilding of the niche behind it. But few take the trouble to go and see Marrina's masterpiece, the altar of the little church of Fontegiusta, or his side altars in San Martino. [*Plate* 41.]

To the left of Marrina's library portal is another very fine piece of Renaissance carving, the Piccolomini altar (1485) by the Milanese artist Andrea Bregno. The five small statues were added a generation later and are attributed with reasonable certainty to Michelangelo, though only the bottom right-hand one is immediately recognizable by

* See page 73.

the layman as his. As the inscription says, this chastely beautiful altar was erected by a nephew of Pius II, one Francesco Piccolomini, Cardinal Archbishop of Siena, who meant to be buried here. But Pius II's nephew was not to die in Siena. The conclave of 1503, meeting to choose a successor to the celebrated Pope Alexander VI (the Borgia), found an ingenious solution to their difficulties. Realizing that it would be several centuries before their late master could expect to receive favourable biographical treatment, and that meanwhile some display of the more self-evident virtues might be advisable (provided the display did not last so long as to become tedious), they chose this provincial prelate whose goodness, learning, moderation, and bad health were a byword. Then it was discovered that the eminent divine who had been archbishop of Siena for the past forty-three years, in fact ever since his uncle appointed him at the promising age of twenty-one, had never been ordained priest. The chain of ceremonies needed to remedy this defect did much to hasten the invalid's end. And so Pius III reigned and died after the briefest of pontificates, 'not disappointing the hopes that had accompanied his election', as a contemporary of his put it. [*Plate* 40.]

We are in his debt for the most captivating thing in Siena, the cathedral library, which he had decorated by Pinturicchio as a memorial to his uncle. Few other relics of the High Renaissance convey, on the first impact, so much of the joy of living in that splendid age. On entering on a sunlit afternoon, when the light is best, one is immediately delighted by the effect of the room as a whole, by its illusion of space, by the freshness and brilliance of the colours which include a generous use of gold. It is only when one examines the ten scenes of Æneas Sylvius' success-story one by one that the costumes, the posturings, the banality, and the gaudiness begin to pall. Berenson, with his dislike of the insubstantial in art, found these charades individually intolerable, but even he ends his paint-blistering comments on Pinturicchio by pointing out what a wonderful piece of interior decoration the room is. Lesser folk would be priggish not to enjoy it. [*Plates* 42, 43.]

Exactly how much the young Raphael helped Pinturicchio in these paintings is disputed. He possibly suggested the general design of some of them—particularly, we are told, the first and fifth of the series. In the foreground of the ninth, on the left, we see the two artists, the young and the old, together.

Puritanical and even practical persons may object that the blaze of colour all down the walls, besides being a distraction from serious reading, leaves very little room indeed for books. But a cathedral library is necessarily specialized, and this one merely conforms in the most elegant manner with the low valuation that the Renaissance set on scholastic theology. Our own age has set out some large illuminated psalters and has prudishly removed the Three Graces in smooth Roman marble, which formerly stood in the middle of this joyful room. They now stand dusty and forlorn in the cathedral museum.

Scots will hasten to examine the second scene, which shows Æneas Sylvius at Edinburgh. This Italian vision of the Scottish Renaissance is, one fears, both premature and unduly flattering. King James' courtiers, who were a murderous lot in fact, look like benign sages, the architecture of his palace shows an improbable degree of refinement, and the sky and the Forth in the background are pellucid. One wonders whether Pinturicchio and Raphael can have read the *Commentaries*.

Of the last age of the Renaissance, before it and Siena died under spiritual thraldom and the mediocrity it bred, not much else is left. The Palazzo del Magnifico next the baptistery, built by Cozzarelli for Pandolfo Petrucci, is now abandoned to damp and squalor and is hardly recognizable as a palace at all. Only the great wrought-iron rings and brackets for flambeaux on the wall suggest that something splendid was once here, and most of them were stolen in the last year of the war. Relics of this palace were scattered before that—there are some charming floor-tiles in the Victoria and Albert Museum. Sienese taste remained good up to the end. The modest triangular Palazzo Pollini by Peruzzi, so modest that its nicely modelled brickwork and clean lines are quite easily overlooked, was the last thing to be designed in free Siena.

9

The Siege

BY EXPELLING CHARLES V's troops in 1552, Siena had only won a short respite. Next year another Spanish army came up from Naples and started operations by investing Montalcino. On this occasion the overworked Queen of Heaven, to whom the Sienese of that generation had twice re-dedicated their state, delegated her ever-recurring task of rescue to the infidels. A Turkish fleet sailed through the Straits of Messina, threatening the Habsburg possessions in southern Italy, to whose defence the hostile army was hastily recalled. As the Spaniards struck their tents and sullenly marched off southwards, the good wives of Montalcino, squawking obscenities and banging saucepan-lids, joined their armed menfolk and the rustic town band on the walls of the little place. In Siena itself, as was fitting in a capital city, the celebrations were more formal and melodious.

In January the imperialists were back again. This time they came down from the north at the instigation of the new Medici tyrant of Florence, Duke Cosimo I. Siena's fate was involved with the fortunes of this ambitious, cold-hearted, competent young man with protruding eyes, whose equestrian statue by Giambologna stands in the Piazza della Signoria at Florence. Bronzino's portrait of him in the Uffizi gives a better idea of his character, and makes one wonder how Filippo Strozzi and the other worthy Florentine democrats, finding their city at last rid of all, however degenerate or illegitimate, who could claim descent in the male line from Cosimo Pater Patriae and Lorenzo il Magnifico, could have been so foolish as to choose this shoot from the junior branch of the Medici tree to be their new nominal head of state. They learned their mistake quickly enough. Within a matter of months the unpleasant young man was dictator of Florence, his foreign *Landsknechte* stood guard in the Loggia dei Lanzi, Filippo Strozzi's colleagues had been tortured and executed as unsuccessful rebels, and Filippo himself murdered in a fortress built at his own expense.

Young Cosimo was quick to climb on to the Habsburg bandwaggon. Charles V, finding him a useful link in his long chain, gave him a dukedom, military guarantees, and his viceroy's daughter in marriage. Not content with the Medici palace where the great Lorenzo had ruled, Cosimo and his family moved first into the Palazzo Vecchio and then into the enormous Palazzo Pitti. Such pretensions could only be made palatable to the Florentines by external successes. And besides, Cosimo was by no means satisfied with a ducal title. He meant to be a king. This last goal eluded him, for neither Charles V nor his successors saw any reason why their satellite in Florence should have such a standing, and by the end of his life Cosimo had only managed to obtain the slightly dubious title of Grand Duke, conferred on him by a venal pope in breach of the imperial prerogative. And the Florentine territory was too small to support even this dignity. He must have all Tuscany.

Free Siena, though small and harmless, stood directly in the path of these ambitions, and Cosimo methodically set himself to subdue a city which Charles V, with more important things to worry about in the year before his abdication, might otherwise have left in peace. In such a case a clever satellite can often get its way. The excuse for the aggression, as in 1260, was the reception by Siena of some Florentine exiles. This time it was Piero Strozzi, Filippo's headstrong son, who to avenge his father's death had gathered a small band of rebels under a flag bearing Dante's great words, '*Libertà vo' cercando*'—'I go seeking freedom.' And so the combined imperial and Florentine forces, largely non-Italian, moved on Siena under the command of another Medici, the marquis of Marignano, an able soldier of fortune. Little more than a fortnight after Strozzi's arrival, the enemy's cavalry were in sight of the Porta Camollia.

At first Marignano's army was too small to invest the city completely. He established himself on the high ground to the north and worked round to the west, occupying Belcaro and the Monistero across the valley. Some skirmishing took place at various scattered places in the *contado*; there was a minor Sienese success at Chiusi.

France was the only ally to which Siena could turn for help, but by this time Henri II was becoming more or less resigned to the Habsburg domination of Italy and was much more interested in the problems of the German frontier. All the same, a foothold in central Italy was worth keeping, both for its nuisance value and for use as a bargaining counter in an eventual settlement with the Empire. Accordingly, in answer to Siena's and Strozzi's appeals, two sizeable bodies of troops were promised. They were to come by sea and land to Viareggio; the combined force was then to move swiftly up the Arno valley and take Florence by surprise. The plan was an excellent one, and in conformance with it Strozzi led his mobile force out of Siena by night, made a quick detour through the hill country to the north-west, and crossed the lower Arno some distance above Pisa. A considerable feat, but unavailing, for owing to the French admiral's jealousy the seaborne contingent failed to make the rendezvous. That jealousy cost them the campaign, for the element of surprise was lost. Strozzi, after waiting some time in vain, crossed the Arno again and eventually met the ships on the coast near Grosseto. Thence the whole army, united too late, moved up to Siena, reinforced by some more Florentine exiles on the way.

With the French troops, at Strozzi's request, came a French general. His task was to command the garrison while Strozzi led his field force outside. Blaise de Montluc had the volatile Gascon temperament. Those in Paris who sent this d'Artagnan to command a mixed assortment of easily offended allies in their own country had serious doubts concerning his suitability—'*parce que j'estois trop bisarre, fascheux & colère,*' he tells us himself—but in fact Montluc's combination of obvious military skill, open-heartedness and panache was exactly right for handling the Sienese. In his *Commentaires*, written in his old age, he has left a sharp-lit picture of free Siena in its last year as seen through an affectionate foreigner's eyes. [*Plate* 44.]

For the last year it was. At the beginning of August, Strozzi led out the field force again, and Marignano followed it. At Marciano, on the edge of the Val di Chiana twenty-five miles to the east, Strozzi insisted on a foolhardy manoeuvre in the face of superior numbers, and his army was destroyed. The wounded survivors spread dismay when they reached Siena. The Spaniards followed and blockaded the city closely. [*Plate* 46.]

Shut up in Siena, Montluc and his captains had leisure and occasion to observe their hosts more closely. It is right to take a last glance at what they saw. To sixteenth-century Frenchmen, brought up on the classics, this little commonwealth looked very much like one of the city-states of antiquity. Here, instead of a hierarchy of royal officials, they found committees of excitable amateurs and shrewd fixers. A fiercely republican spirit replaced the mystique of service to a throne, and of honour flowing from it. With free parties, though with no developed parliament and little separation of powers, this enclave in late Renaissance Italy had a good deal more in common with the Athens of Demosthenes than with the France of Henri II, or for that matter with a modern nation-state. Would-be democracies on so small a scale are likely to evolve along broadly the same lines at any period, especially in the Mediterranean. In a city-state, where family ties are all-important and everyone knows everyone else, representative institutions as we know them would seem far too impersonal and rigid. Siena and Athens shared a comparable social development with a gradual broadening of citizenship (always leaving a good many inhabitants disfranchised), a comparable constant happy tinkering with the constitution, a comparable imperialism on somewhat harsh and unimaginative lines, and even a comparable interlocking of patriotism and religion—both states were greatly strengthened by the mystical guardianship of a Virgin. Of course there were differences. The Sienese had neither the Greek institution of slavery nor the Greek curiosity and independence of mind. Even so, Montluc and his captains could see before them the main features of a classical *polis*.

Montluc himself, whose favourite classical reading-matter was Livy at his most heroic, thought of his hosts as Romans rather than as Greeks. '*Que vous estes les vrays enfans legitimes de ces anciens Romains belliqueux,*' he was always telling them. His book was written as a sort of Staff College text-book, and the story of how he defended Siena is constantly being broken off to allow of military generalizations, *Instructions pour les Gouverneurs des places* and *Remonstrances aux capitaines*, in which future generations of French commanders are strongly advised to heed his illustrious example. For Montluc was not a Gascon for nothing; his book is a sustained solo on his own trumpet; and only once do we find among the many editorial sub-headings in the margin, drawing attention to passages in which he extolls his '*Bel ordre pour la conservation d'une place*', his

'*Prudence*', '*Ruses*', '*Inventions*', '*Sage advis*', and '*Belles considerations*', the entry, '*Faute du Sieur de Montluc*'. This last refers to his omission to send the 'useless mouths' out of the town before it was completely surrounded.

One should not laugh at Montluc more than he laughs at himself. He was a very brave man. He knew, better than the Sienese, just how desperate the siege was going to be and how little hope there was of a relieving army coming out from France to raise it. More-ever he was seriously ill. He had not been well before he left home, and his doctors had opposed his going. On the day he arrived he hurled himself into a brisk skirmish near the convent St. Catherine founded, restoring a difficult situation. A fortnight later he was down with high fever and dysentery, though this did not stop him from struggling up to the Palazzo and giving the city fathers the first of his celebrated harangues, in which he warned them to expect bad news from Strozzi and to look to their own defences more strictly. Soon after that he became very ill indeed, and the doctors despaired of saving him. When Strozzi came to Siena some weeks afterwards, he found him out of danger but so thin that the bones stuck through his skin in several places. Fortunately the enemy did not attack the city until he had recovered.

Strozzi made a dash through the enemy lines, returning to his base at Montalcino, where he hoped to be able to help more than by staying in the town. Montluc, rising painfully from his bed, had himself carried round the defences in a chair and looked over the battlements approvingly at *les belles escarmouches* which went on daily outside. He found the people *bien resolus de garder leur liberté* and pays tribute to their loyalty and courage; whenever there came a call to arms, not a single man, young or old, remained at home. Their leaders he handled, at each crisis in the siege, by going to the Palazzo Pubblico and delivering a harangue, no fewer than six of which he sets down at full length for the edification of posterity. Although it is not entirely improbable that the words of this close student of Livy as we have them represent what he would have liked to have said, rather than what he did say, speeches like these must be judged by their results, and they clearly served his purpose of encouraging the Sienese to prolong resistance as long as possible. He spoke in Italian at the time, he tells us, but in his book he gives his orations in French so that the Gascon country gentlemen who will read it may have no excuse for skipping these passages.

No doubt they re-read several times the gallant author's praise of the Sienese ladies.

> 'It shall never be, you Ladies of Siena, that I will not immortalize your names so long as the Book of Montluc shall live; for in truth you are worthy of immortal praise, if ever women were. At the beginning of the noble resolution these people took to defend their liberty, all the ladies of Siena divided themselves into three squadrons; the first led by Signora Forteguerra, who was herself clad in violet, as also those of her train, her attire being cut in the fashion of a Nymph, short, and discovering her buskins: the second was the Signora Piccolomini, attired in carnation satin, and her troop in the same livery; the third was the Signora Livia Fausta, apparelled all in white, as also her train, with her white ensign. In their ensigns they had very fine devices, which I would

give a good deal I could remember. These three squadrons consisted of three thousand ladies, gentlewomen and citizens; their arms were picks, shovels, baskets and bavins; and in this equipage they made their muster, and went to begin the fortifications.'*

But that was at the start of the siege. Soon it became more serious. Peasants who tried to bring food or to drive cattle into the city were hanged by the enemy within sight of the walls. As Montluc himself remarks, soldiers come through war better than civilians. Our own age has not banished the anomaly, it has only, in the name of a people's war, cut down the gestures of courtesy between opposing generals. For these last, in 1554, there were advantages. On Christmas Eve Marignano sent Montluc half a roebuck, three brace of capons and of partridges, six bottles of excellent wine, and six loaves of white bread. He had also allowed some medicines from Florence to reach him, as well as a mule from Rome loaded with little flagons of Greek wine, which Montluc had asked for when he was delirious, and which a friendly cardinal had sent him as a present. Half of these flagons were distributed to nursing mothers, Strozzi got some, and of the rest the general made good use.

Marignano's politeness was not free from duplicity, for that night he attacked the forts near the Porta Camollia, and managed to get a foothold inside them. But in our hero's margin we read the reassuring heading, '*Le Sieur de Montluc au secours*', and the forts were promptly re-taken. A second enemy attack in the early hours failed, for the Spaniards unaccountably carried torches as they advanced, making a perfect target for Montluc's two French guns and two hundred Sienese arquebusiers. As daylight came and the enemy withdrew, Montluc collapsed and was carried to his quarters.

After some acid exchanges with his employers, Marignano now sent to Florence for heavy artillery, and soon the town learned with consternation that twenty-six or more pieces were on their way. This called for another harangue in the Palazzo and an extra degree of sartorial care. Rising once more from his sick-bed, Montluc put on his best clothes, which he had had the foresight to bring with him and not to wear till this moment. They had been specially made for him when he was courting a lady during a spell of garrison duty in the north of Italy, when he had unwonted leisure, *& n'ayant rien à faire il le faut donner aux Dames*. Though a little unfashionable now, the clothes were still very fine. He rubbed his face vigorously with some of the cardinal's Greek wine, drank a little, and ate a small roll of bread. '*Puis me regarday au miroir. Je vous jure, que je ne me cognoissois pas moy mesme, & me sembloit que j'estois encore en Piedmont amoureux, comme j'avois esté.*' Thus renewed, he rode to the Palazzo with his officers and made his speech. Was it possible that Sienese hearts, hearts so generous, should have taken fright on hearing this talk of artillery? Had they then decided to make themselves the slaves of this insupportable nation the Spaniards, or of their neighbours and old enemies? Did they think it possible that this sickness should have impaired his own military prowess? Would His Most Christian Majesty have sent them a general in whom he lacked confidence? It was one of his best *Remonstrances*, and the Signory, quite carried away, re-

* Cotton's translation (1674), from E. Gardner, *op. cit.*, p. 234.

solved again to resist to the last, while Montluc went out to go his rounds, showing townsmen and soldiers by his cheerful demeanour that he wished for nothing better than an immediate assault by the enemy.

He was not only a morale-builder. Looking at Siena's topography, he saw a way to meet the threat of Marignano's artillery. Instead of defending whichever section of the walls the enemy bombarded, his plan was to clear a field of fire immediately behind it, building lateral defences quickly at right angles to the ramparts while the latter were being breached. All available fire-power was to be concentrated round the sides of this trap or *retirade*, as he called it—on each side *quatre ou cinq grosses pieces d'artillerie, chargées de grosses chaisnes & de gros cloux & pieces de fer*, and, at the back, parallel with the breached rampart, *tous les mousquets de la ville, ensemble l'arquebuzerie*. In this way he hoped to inflict such losses as would compel Marignano to raise the siege, for he saw no other way out in the long run.

Montluc envisaged this happening in one of those deep cleughs or re-entrants within the walls but outside the built-up area. Unfortunately, the enemy sited their battery on rising ground, now recently built over, near the Porta Ovile. Here, inside the town, the houses nearly touched the walls. It was that unquiet weavers' quarter of the Caterpillar. But the inhabitants had kept something of their militant *trecento* spirit, and, to Montluc's surprise, helped in the deliberate destruction of their homes without grumbling. The Sienese, little touched by the prevailing political corruption of the time, were still a people, not a population.

The guns began to batter the curtain wall between the Porta Ovile, with its projecting *antiporta*, and the high-set Franciscan friary, while the defenders worked energetically at strengthening these two positions as the forward angles of their *retirade*. Then Montluc seems to have overreached himself and to have spoiled his own plan. He brought up one gun, manned by a local gunner, and opened counter-battery fire. *Et fist ce Siennois de si grands coups, qu'il leur démonta six pieces de canon; & demeura leur artillerie toute abandonée.* One shot knocked down the wall of a cottage close to Marignano himself, who was *si estonné* that, as he told Montluc afterwards, the shock completely cured his gout. That night the Spaniards withdrew the rest of their guns. At daybreak the delighted Sienese, seeing the empty gun-sites, stood up on top of the rampart and shouted after the enemy an indelicate expression that can still be heard in the streets of the Caterpillar district.

Poveri ragazzi, they shouted too soon. The Spaniards now decided to let starvation do their work. Supplies in the town were already desperately low. Noticing that his contingent of German mercenaries ate more than the others, and that they were growing restive under the reduced rations, Montluc made them fight their way out, for food was a worse problem than man-power. Then he proposed that all civilians whose presence could not be justified militarily should leave the city too. The Signory could not bring themselves to give this order, but conferred powers on Montluc to do what he thought right. The commission he appointed drew up a list of 4,400 *bocche disutili* or *bouches inutiles*, including many women and all the children from the Hospital, whose rector resigned in protest. Both Montluc and Sienese sources have left ghastly descriptions of what happened when they were sent out. Most of them perished between the city walls and the enemy lines.

A modest fall of snow, which was not unusual at this time of year, might have saved the town, for Marignano's army had eaten up everything for twenty miles around, his supply-line from Florence was breaking down—why did not Strozzi disrupt it?—and a little extra hardship would have forced the enemy to raise the siege. The snow did not come. An agent of Marignano's tried to sow dissention between the *monti* by fabricating evidence of treachery against leading citizens. Montluc withstood the general panic, saved the lives of the accused, and unmasked the agent. He even saved him from execution too. He organized penitential processions through the town, which was once more re-dedicated to the Madonna. The Signory appealed to Pope Julius III to mediate on behalf of his mother's city, but he refused; *c'estoit un terrible Pape*. By the end of March soldiers and inhabitants were literally starving. The last hens that laid eggs for the headquarters mess had been eaten, and the cock too. Even cats at four scudi and rats at a quarter the price had all gone. An almost exclusive diet of boiled mallows, picked along the walls at some danger, proved after a time to be poisonous. People fell down dead in the street. The struggle was over.

At Montluc's insistence, the terms of the capitulation protected not only his own troops but the Sienese civilians and the Florentine exiles, rebels against Duke Cosimo and the Empire, as well. On 21 April 1555 the garrison marched out of the Porta Romana, under arms and with standards unfurled, and were given the honours of war and free passage to Montalcino, which was to remain under French protection. Marignano met Montluc three hundred yards beyond the gate. They embraced, and the ice broke at the first exchange of compliments; they rode along together, happily talking over the military details of the siege like the professionals they were. Each claimed to have been cured by the other of fever or of gout. The irrepressible Gascon pointed out a tactical error committed by the marquis, who quietly promised to be wiser next time. After two miles Marignano asked Montluc to recommend him humbly to the king of France, and they parted. At Ponte a Tressa Montluc's men found bread, provided by the Spaniards, and halted by the edge of the stream under the willows to eat their first substantial meal for a long time. For them an uncomfortable episode was well over. *Car les gens de guerre passent par tout: & tousiours avec meillieure marché que les autres.*

But with them plodded a column of over eight hundred refugees, Sienese civilians, men, women, and children, with babies in cradles and old women on pack-mules lent by Marignano—those who refused to become the subjects of his less humane master the duke, and who carried the Sienese Republic with them to live on at Montalcino, until this tiny state-in-exile too was extinguished by the European treaty four years later. Montluc was moved to tears. *Oncques en ma vie je n'ay veu despartie si desolée . . . regrettant infiniment ce peuple, qui s'estoit monstré si devotieux à sauver sa liberté.*

Despite the worthy and often happy lives of many succeeding generations, nothing really memorable has been done in Siena since they left.

10

Outside Siena

'The sweet season of spring had come, and all the hills about Siena stood smiling, clothed with leafy trees and flowers, and in the fields the crops were springing up in generous growth. For the country which lies within sight of the city of Siena is more lovely than can be told. Gently rising hills, planted with orchards and vines or ploughed for grain, overlook pleasant valleys, bright with young corn or grass and never without a running brook. Moreover there are many woods and copses where the birds sing most sweetly, nor is there any height which has not been splendidly crowned by a gentleman's country house. On one hill stands a noble monastery, the dwelling of holy men, and on the next, a private mansion built like a stronghold. Through these parts the Pontiff travelled in great good humour . . .'

ON A MAY morning in 1460 Pius II, finding the streets of Siena suddenly too small for him, assembled a cortège as modest as protocol allowed and went out of one of the gates into the gracious countryside beyond, leaving us this record of the relief he felt. What would he have thought of the same streets today? It is safe to say that the youths without silencers on their motor-scooters would have been excommunicated on the spot. Reflecting sadly that a satisfactory solution of Siena's modern traffic problem might defy even the powers of a Renaissance pope, we may at least follow his example and escape for a time from a city which, lovely as it is, can easily produce in Northerners the symptoms of advanced claustrophobia.

The Sienese landscape is highly civilized in the best sense of the word. Its more fertile stretches have been cultivated intensively but sanely for something not far short of three thousand years and everything there, however attractive to the eye, is practical too, so that even the castles suggest the military engineering of their day rather than romance. It is precisely this functional, classic character of the country that appealed to Æneas Sylvius, and that remains its chief attraction today.

Looked at more closely, the Sienese landscape reveals itself as the product of pliocene geology, medieval insecurity, *mezzadria* land tenure, the ornamental proclivities of past landowners, and of slow patient skills like vine-tending and olive-pruning.

The geology is 'recent' and somewhat complicated. Much of the country is composed of layers of sandstone or *tufo* and of soft grey marl, with occasional outcrops of harder rock, like the yellowish marble found in the Montagnola or the silvery grey travertine quarried extensively south of Rapolano. The travertine is ideal for masonry, though the easier cut *tufo* hardens well on exposure and, but for its rather untaking yellow-ochre colour, makes quite a good building stone. For some miles immediately round Siena, except to the south, the *tufo* predominates, producing a pleasant confusion of hills, often steep-sided but clothed with orchards and olive trees and no more than a few hundred feet above the twisting courses of the little valleys—in fact the fertile, diversified terrain that met with papal commendation. The *tufo*, on a deep stratum of which the city itself is built, also acts as a useful shock-absorber for earth-tremors; softer rock would have split into faults and on harder rock the tall buildings would have been shaken down.

To the north-east, as limestone replaces the *tufo*, these moderate hills rise gradually until they grow into the Chianti ridges, with thin woods and a litter of boulders on the summits, and the vineyards all down the lower slopes. To the west the Montagnola and Monte Maggio, outliers of the wild Colline Metallifere, rise more abruptly, unblest by vines. Between these two blocks of hill country runs the main road north-west, dropping down into the Val d'Elsa and soon passing out of Sienese territory into that of Florence.

Some of the villages are strung lucklessly along the roads, a succession of sharp dust-smothered corners and stringy Darwinian chickens, but there is an older pattern which tends to perch on top of the steepest hill available and which takes the form of a tight cluster of houses, continuous round the outer edge. The old defensive wall has virtually disappeared by incorporation in the outer ring of houses, but one or more simple gateways remain. This kind of village, confusingly called a *castello*,* is of course a consequence of the never-ending passage of predatory armies through this rich but divided countryside. Even now that it has lost its military advantages, the inhabitants find it companionable and cool in summer, and show little sign of leaving. Instead they call loudly for better roads and piped water, and rather surprisingly are beginning to get them.

The farms, even those built recently, often follow this ancient preference for a high site. The overwhelming majority are run on the *mezzadria* system, the Tuscan form of share-cropping, in which the landlord (or his factor) has the last word on the year's plan, maintains buildings and roads, advances money, shares running costs and, instead of rent, takes half the year's produce. A recent law has raised the tenant's share to 53 per cent, while increased local taxes and social contributions have likewise reduced the landlord's takings. This old-established system is now working less well than it used to. Theoretically it is an excellent tenure, being a form of profit-sharing which does not reduce most of the farming population to the status of labourers, and which should enable capital for development to be found more easily than it can be by small self-sufficient tenants or peasant proprietors. But now the share-cropper or *mezzadro*, in a world of rising living standards and changing social values, no longer regards the ratio

* A ruined castle is usually known as a *rocca*.

as equitable, and has taken to sit-down strikes and left-wing politics to say so, while the landowner hesitates to plough back his profits into an enterprise thus threatened. There is considerable dissatisfaction all round, but the alternative of large-scale direct farming accompanied by chronic labour troubles is even less attractive. So *mezzadria*, with its scope for never-ending argument and readjustment, is likely to continue for some time to come, though slowly giving place to peasant ownership or estate farming.

The Tuscan landowner lives more often in his town house than in his country villa and in consequence is, by and large, a more cultured and less hardy specimen than his British equivalent. But he is by no means wholly an absentee from his estate and, when there, has an eye for beauty greatly more creative than that of the average peasant or public authority. It is he who has planted those tellingly sited cypresses grouped on hill-tops or lining farm tracks along ridges, and his villa, of whatever period, is almost always marked by character rather than pretentiousness. For these things the British traveller, however radical his social sympathies may become when he goes abroad, should be duly grateful.

The peasants, though socially restive, are friendly, and in this part of the country, whose dialect grew into received Italian, one can understand what they say. Nobody coming from a land where husbandry consists mainly in towing some multi-purpose machinery behind a tractor can watch their age-old methods unmoved. Terraces must be laboriously restored after the rains. Every new vine-shoot calls for individual judgement. The small plough behind the white oxen is urged, a few steps at a time, along a steep slope between the boles of olive trees. It is craftsmanship. But surely, one thinks, it must be utterly uneconomic? The answer is that the terrain and the crop do not allow of mechanization, that no substitute is likely to be found for wine, and that even the adulterated fluid that is now used in Italian and other frying-pans must, to be palatable, still contain a fairly high proportion of olive oil.

But it is time to get out into this country. Unfortunately, the first mile outside the gates has become a zone of motor-roads, haphazard blocks of flats, small factories and depressing *terrains vagues*, though this peripheral clutter is on a much less extensive scale than it is outside most towns of similar size, and the worst of it is hidden out of sight in deep valleys. But the way out to Florence has been ruined, so that the little pillar seen in Pinturicchio's fresco, which marks the spot where Frederick III met his Portuguese bride and was then in an idyllic rural setting, is now lost among featureless semi-modernity. Some way farther out on this road, just before the Palazzo dei Diavoli with its rather naïve Renaissance decorations, one turns off to the left, and at Poggio al Vento finds oneself at last outside the town. Here is the small Villa Paoletti, now an orphanage, where Robert and Elizabeth Browning passed two summers. One can still look out from the terraced garden over the view of which she wrote: 'The whole country leaps under the sun, alive with verdure and vineyards.' [*Plate* 47.]

A vantage-point easier reached, with a less intimate but wider view, is outside the Porta San Marco, and from here one can set out to the imposing villas of the Monistero and Belcaro on hilltops opposite. Belcaro in particular is in unspoilt country, well off the main roads, and has a splendid prospect of the city something over two miles away as the crow flies but much more than that on foot. In the other direction, a good mile beyond the Porta Ovile, is the convent of the Osservanza, founded by San Bernardino for that reformed branch of the Franciscans who wished to observe their founder's rule in something approaching its original strictness. The church, with a pleasant clean Renaissance interior by Cozzarelli, was badly damaged in 1944 by bombs intended for the railway station. It has been well restored and contains a Della Robbia and several pictures of some interest, in particular one by the Master of the Osservanza, an elusive personality reassembled by modern cunning out of a jig-saw of works previously ascribed to Sassetta and Sano. But the view looking back to the city at sunset, so deservedly praised in the past, has suffered from recent building in between.

Beyond here too is a country of moderate slopes, vineyards and orchards, villas and meandering lanes. Among the villas is Quattro Torri, a well-restored fifteenth-century castle prominently visible from any tower or high balcony in the town. Farther out is the former Carthusian monastery of Pontignano with its three deserted cloisters, lifeless but for the soft insistent question of the little southern owl or *chiù*. [*Plate* 52.]

The visitor with a car at his disposal or the weather and will for a long walk would do better to go outside this limited radius. A mile or two beyond Belcaro there is an area of pleasant low stony hills covered with holm-oaks. These dry woods, not unlike those of the Dordogne in France and full of wild flowers in spring, are the *lecce* or ilexes of Lecceto, where that good man William Flete so sensibly preferred to stay in daily contact with something better and holier than the tantrums of a dubiously elected and correspondingly uncharitable pope. In the forecourt of the abandoned monastery, once the mother house of the Augustinian hermits and a great centre of religious influence in the district, is a much damaged fresco of the mid-*trecento* by Paolo di Maestro Neri, showing the path of the worldly leading by way of dalliance and warfare and other activities to hell; the path that leads in the other direction has been too much washed away by time to yield any certain information. One's impression of it all is more of lovely faded colours than of objects or composition. This fresco is said to have influenced Fra Filippo's *Assempri* or *Examples*, a collection of moralizing tales written in this monastery a generation later. It also doubtless strengthened William Flete's sound Cambridge aversion to the vanity of lost causes. In fact he found even this quiet place too distracting, and perhaps too easily reached by St. Catherine, and retired with some other hermits to the smaller priory of San Leonardo al Lago at the northern edge of the wood. Here the lake has long been reclaimed for cultivation, and now the commissioners for ancient monuments are industriously restoring the frescoes and finding new ones. It is to be hoped that they do not furbish up the sleepy little place too much. It should remain for individual discovery and pilgrimage.

Some four or five miles still further westwards one reaches the Montagnola, a range of hills approaching 2,000 feet, whose quiet byroads winding up through high chestnut woods to marble quarries and minute wood-cutters' clachans are very well worth exploring. There are tiny Romanesque churches scattered through these hills. From its position near the top the mock-Gothic Villa Celsa has a remarkable view towards Siena, and at the foot are some other aristocratic villas, of which the best known is Cetinale, an attractive Baroque building surrounded by landscape gardening and over-sized statues. For the visitor with limited time and average tastes this is the best direction in which to explore.

Hereabouts, in the open plain just below Sovicille, is the best Romanesque church within easy reach of Siena, the Pieve di Ponte allo Spino. It has a tall interior of admirable proportions and is altogether a model of what a smaller twelfth-century church should be. Four miles to the south, past the good Romanesque campanile of the otherwise most undistinguished village of Rosía, is the *castello* or fortified hamlet of Torri. Next the church is a perfect little cloister of the same period with slender columns and delightfully carved capitals. It has been converted into the courtyard of a villa, but visitors are usually admitted. This is a thing that should not be missed, and the setting of the place between the hills and the plain is one of the most beautiful in the whole district.

On the far side of the Montagnola, approached through the defile of Rosía, is a fresh landscape of woods and hills and red earth. Here the best place to make for is Mensano, a remote village on a pinnacle in the Colline Metallifere, approached latterly by a corkscrew byroad. The view over the wild empty country is like one from an aeroplane, and the early eleventh-century church, with its bottle-shaped pillars, good capitals, and alabaster window-slits, is probably the finest village church in Tuscany. [*Plate* 48.]

Going out from Siena in the opposite direction, one comes to the battlefield of Montaperti. It does not deserve a special visit, but the driver on his way eastwards to Arezzo or Chiusi, after he has crossed the Arbia and the railway some seven kilometres from the Porta Píspini and is making good speed along the rather featureless road beyond, finds himself on the line where the Florentines stood to face the Sienese main body across the stream and were thrown into confusion by an unexpected attack from behind the rising ground to their rear. The battle is named illogically, after the manner of battles, from the place a mile and a half further north where the pursuit stopped, well beyond the chapel of Sant' Ansano where the eighth-century Sienese interrupted that episcopal burglary. On the steep knowe of Montaperti, which was then topped by a castle and is now marked by a prominent group of cypresses and a monument, the enemy made their last stand. Their cumbersome headquarters vehicles, the *carroccio* and the other one with the bell, could not retreat across country and were captured somewhere near the roadside.

Northwards the main road to Florence takes one past the Sienese outpost of Monteriggioni, a perfect diadem of towers against the sky, with olives and vines spreading down the slopes below. Dante found the sight alarming. [*Plate* 49.]

Però che, come in su la cerchia tonda
Montereggion di torri si corona
cosi la proda che il pozzo circonda
torreggiavan di mezza la persona
gli orribili giganti, cui minaccia
Giove del cielo ancora, quando tuona.

. . .As with circling round
Of turrets, Montereggion crowns his walls;
E'en thus the shore, encompassing the abyss,
Was turreted with giants, half their length
Uprearing, horrible, whom Jove from heaven
Yet threatens, when his muttering thunder rolls.*

Today Monteriggioni makes one think of a peaceful, bright little scene from a Book of Hours, and it takes an effort to recapture Dante's mood. To him these towers must have had the associations of concrete dragons' teeth on the Channel coast.

Further on is Staggia, another fortified place in this disputed borderland. A square wall surrounds the village and there is the imposing ruin of a castle at one corner. In this castle the French king's agent Nogaret stayed in 1303 and methodically wove his net of intrigue round Boniface VIII. And how 'modern' was the social structure of medieval Tuscany; his host at the time, far from being a great feudal lord, was the banker Musciatto Francesi, the confidential man of business who looked after French financial interests in the peninsula.

To the right of this road to Florence, the main artery running through the district, rise the high limestone hills of Chianti, whence the straw-covered flagons are sent out all over the world. The comely traditional shape contains an equally traditional blend from four varieties of grape in different proportions, improved by a second fermentation, a blend which enables the consumer to rely on a good average standard without worrying about localities and years. Makers' names are more important. Those who take wine-drinking seriously should confine their attentions to Chianti Classico, whose symbol is the black cock on the label; it comes from this restricted area alone, though inferior wines from as much as fifty miles away may call themselves Chianti. Compared with other famous wine countries, the Chianti hills are austere and a little disappointing, though a clean landscape matches a clean drink. The market towns of Castellina and Radda are uncompromising, stone-built, grim little places, and even the Castello di Brolio, a great name on a label, is nothing much to look at, apart from its grove of giant cypresses.

Turning left at Monteriggioni and left again on to a byroad after a mile or so, the former Benedictine abbey church of Badia a Isola is found embedded among mellow farm buildings. Standing behind the apse, one can realize how it must have looked when the water of the lake almost lapped against it. But the lake has long been drained, leaving nothing of the island but a slight rise in the ground and the watery rhythm of the name. The church, founded by Ava countess of Tuscany in the year 1001, is being restored and in part rebuilt as it once was. It is an ambitious enterprise and will take some time. It is to be hoped they will not spoil it with the bad stained glass, neither traditional nor reputably modern, which is the chief fault of church-restorers in these parts. There is a fresco by Vecchietta, but what one comes to see, of course, is the great *Virgin* by Duccio.

* *Inferno*, 31, 41–46 (Cary's translation).

No one who has to any degree 'discovered' him in Siena should miss it. After a great deal of learned argument it is now accepted as one of his early works, painted before 1285 while he was still fairly close to Cimabue. The false perspective of the throne and its steps is the kind of thing that the cubists spent years trying to do and, though Duccio himself did not mean it so, it helps to lift the modern spectator on to another plane of consciousness and to make him surrender to the timeless, brooding influence of this gold-webbed archetypal figure. When the builders have finished it will look most effective against the restored Romanesque apse, placed as Duccio intended it to be—provided, of course, that one will be able to see it properly. [*Plate* 51.]

A few miles further down the road is Colle di Val d'Elsa, an ugly little place in the valley, its old bridge gone, full of small factories making paper and glass, and possessing a ghastly square only redeemed by the weekly market. The upper and older part of Colle qualifies as a hill-town and, seen from the road to Volterra which by-passes it to the north, looks quite worth exploring. But it scarcely repays the labour, even for Dante specialists in search of that hubristic lady Sapia who loudly defied God and the Ghibellines from its ramparts.* There are a few ancient *case-torri*, a quiet and not unattractive piazza by the undistinguished cathedral, one or two modest *palazzi* and no more. The guide-books and some writers who should know better send one panting out several kilometres to look for the abbey of Coneo, but there is less to be seen there than in most of these Romanesque churches.

Even more do these strictures apply to Poggibonsi. The nicest thing about it is its name, suggesting fat little flagons, for it is on the edge of the Chianti country and women sit on their doorsteps plaiting the straw covers. Apart from this cottage industry it is a dreary little town, one of those where innumerable men, all with hats worn absolutely straight on their heads, stand talking in the street for hours on end and only stop to look at any stranger with the bovine glare of a Soviet statesman's bodyguard.

Both of these places were important bones of contention in the *duecento*. Colle, geographically closer to Siena, inclined to Florence. Poggibonsi was more independent and stood several sieges, until finally, as that chauvinist Villani tells us: 'On account of their pride, because they wished to go their own way as a castle of the Empire and to stand out against the commune of Florence, it was thrown down and deprived by the Florentines of all its jurisdiction.' This was in 1270. A new town arose in the less defensible valley. On the heights to the south, beyond the Medicean fortifications, is the abbey church of San Lucchese, founded by a repentant Sienese banker and his wife, who on meeting St. Francis became the first tertiaries of his order. It is a good example of a Franciscan church of the end of the thirteenth century, and contains a few things of moderate interest such as a Della Robbia side-altar and a fresco by Bartolo di Fredi. Here we see St. Nicholas saving three sisters, who are in bed, from a fate worse than death—*per condurre ad onor lor giovinezza*, as Dante puts it less hypocritically than the Victorians.

South of Siena the landscape changes abruptly as the sandstone gives place to grey

* *Purgatorio*, 13, 106 ff.

clay or *creta*. The woods and orchards disappear, the hills recede, and the view opens out into something like an Italian version of Salisbury Plain—slow curves and ridges of corn-land, empty save for meandering lines of poplars and pollarded willows along the watercourses below, and a scattering of brown blocks and dark flicks on the skyline, where farms and cypresses emphasize every hump.

This *creta* country has a great deal of character and has lately been re-discovered by a few discerning contemporary painters, but the motorist driving towards Rome will find nothing to arouse his curiosity, unless he turns off the almost featureless main road. In fact the first few miles are most discouraging. Once outside the Porta Romana all throttles are opened to their fullest extent, and the traffic gathers speed between straggling dusty houses with permanently intimidated inhabitants and the vile hoardings which Italian commercial interests put up to deter all but the most insensitive of their clients. You flash past Malamerenda, whose story of eighteen members of the Tolomei clan slaughtered at a banquet by their enemies the Salimbeni carries one's mind for a moment to similar sites in the Highlands, before it is hastily recalled to the road by more immediate chances of sudden death. Through ugly little places like Ponte a Tressa, dejected communities which the traffic cuts in half as with a knife blade. The Sienese expression for a local youth of unconvincing pretensions is *un Inglesino sbarcato a Tressa*, a young English milord who has landed from his yacht at this most unnautical of places. Past several petrol-stations and the large new tower of a tomato-purée factory. Why the tower? Can it be that they drop the tomatoes down the inside to make their product? No one seems to know or care. Away to the right is a huge medieval granary which belonged to the Hospital, but the fast approaching bottleneck of Monteroni claims all one's attention. Presently the road gets clear of all this, but follows a scenically unexciting course along the river valley, mercifully leaving on one side the hamlet of Lucignano d'Arbia, where the newly found Simone Martini came from and whose classically simple monuments the writer's uncle, Senatore Alfredo Bruchi, did much to preserve. Soon the road is skirting Buonconvento, with its tall gateway and its rectangular ground-plan like that of a *bastide* in south-western France, but with nothing else to commend it except the memory that Dante's German emperor died here.

At this point the knowledgeable will turn to the left and take the byroad leading to Asciano. Within a mile the *creta* country begins to reveal its fascination. As the car turns and climbs, first the abrupt folds and then the bare bones of this terrain are spread before one. Landslips and precipices of clay fall from the roadside into deep ravines. The road clings to the hilltops and clambers along the narrow necks connecting them. On a spur near the summit stands the long bulk of Monte Oliveto Maggiore, the mother house of the Olivetan order or White Benedictines, founded by Bernardo Tolomei and two other Sienese patricians who renounced the world in 1313. The site was a fantastic desert until the monks planted olives and giant cypresses and so made the oasis that one sees today. [*Plates* 50, 53.]

The gate-tower, adorned with Della Robbias, is the only thing older than the sixteenth century. The remote high site, the white robes, the featureless corridors, and the impression of strictness are a bit unnerving at first. Somehow there is an almost Tibetan feeling about this monastery. One dutifully admires the choir-stalls, thaws a little in the library and the pharmacy, and finds contact in the *clinica del libro*, a most interesting place where ancient books, apparently defaced, worm-eaten and even charred beyond all hope, are restored by modern techniques to a state in which they can be looked at with enjoyment.

All round the cloister are the frescoes illustrating the legend of St. Benedict. Signorelli began work on them in 1497, starting perhaps rather desperately in the middle of the saint's life. The prescribed episodes were as tediously edifying as a Victorian child's Sunday reading-matter, and into every would-be dynamic pattern the cream-coloured habits of the monks introduced an awkward, static element. Signorelli did what he could along most of one wall. Then the thought that this cycle had to stretch slowly round three more sides of the cloister was too much for him, and he abandoned the task for a more congenial and imaginative one at Orvieto. Sodoma finished the job some years later, bringing his private indoor menagerie with him to help him keep sane. Vasari, in his *Lives of the Painters*, speaks with aversion of the 'badgers, squirrels, apes, cat-a-mountains, dwarf asses, horses and barbs to run races, magpies, dwarf chickens, tortoises, Indian doves and other animals', as well as a raven with a gift for vocal mimicry, 'insomuch as the dwelling of this man seemed like the very Ark of Noah'. Vasari does not like Sodoma. 'Coarse, licentious and eccentric as he was, he had acquired the reputation of being one who wasted his time with infinite levity and with idle young men, and was even willing to accept that character.' At least he had the perseverence to finish St. Benedict's life, twenty-seven scenes in all, not counting Signorelli's.

Where Signorelli's treatment had been broad and experimental, Sodoma's was facile and sugary; the delicate backgrounds and the many small details, such as birds and animals, are more worth looking at than the repetitive, self-conscious figures. Among these last the youths have come in for most criticism. 'His young men are fleshy at the knee,' barks the robust Mr. Langton Douglas. 'They look as though they would have been the better for a month or two of hard training.' '*Ces adolescents par trop équivoques*,' sighs the more worldly M. du Colombier.

The abbot bore all this disruption of monastic routine with patience, so long as St. Benedict's banal miracles continued to march steadily on round the cloister walls in an acceptable form. But the monotony of the series got on Sodoma's nerves too, as it does on ours today, and in a late scene he suddenly confronted the saint and his monks with a strip-tease act in its final stage. For this temptation there was indeed warrant in the legend, but the abbot, his pastoral cares overcoming logic, insisted that it should be lessened by a flurry of draperies, supplied reluctantly by the painter. Some caricatures of the brothers at Monte Oliveto had to go too, but Sodoma's complacent self-portrait, dressed up to the nines and with his raven and his badgers at his feet, was allowed to stand. [*Plate* 54.]

Up here the *creta* country has lost any resemblance it had to Salisbury Plain and has become the stark precipitous landscape seen in the backgrounds of many Sienese pictures. Here and there bushes and trees have been planted to hold the slopes from slipping further, but for miles around, and towards Siena in particular, erosion is still attacking the hills like woodworm. It is a landscape in full decay. The rains first mould it into countless rounded hummocks, large and small, and then tear it apart into ragged putty-coloured cliffs. After that the sun comes out and bakes it hard. A lot has been done to reclaim it for agriculture, but the higher reaches practically defy human intervention. There is no need to go out as far as Monte Oliveto to see it; the roads from Siena or Monteroni to Asciano have plenty to show; and no one whose taste in landscape inclines to the dry rather than the sweet should neglect to walk over the lonely ridges round the hilltop farm of Montacuto on a spring morning.

To enter Asciano armed with a travel book of the last generation is to experience a severe shock. Can this drab, fly-blown straggle of houses ever have constituted a place 'to be loved for her own sake . . . one of the most charming of all those delightful towns that lie like flowers on the skirts of Siena'? Local people, whose memory goes back to 1910, discount the description as over-lyrical even at the time when it was written. Today, at any rate, Asciano is a dump, to be driven through as fast as considerations of safety and charity towards the luckless inhabitants permit, at most stopping briefly to look at one remarkable picture. For what few paintings the various damp churches once contained have quite sensibly been collected in an unpretentious museum of sacred art, where they have better prospects of survival and can be seen without eyestrain, semi-blasphemous clamberings on ill-lit altars, or the fumblings of garrulous custodians with the wrong keys. The painting that stands out among them is Ambrogio Lorenzetti's *St. Michael and the Dragon*, an extraordinary work for its period, a whirlwind figure more than Baroque in its dash and fantasy, and wearing a helmet that might almost be Japanese. Anyone who thinks that Sienese *trecento* painting is too stereotyped should come to Asciano and see this picture. After that, as the inn that comforted Edwardians no longer exists, he should take his leave.

11

San Gimignano

THERE ARE PLACES which gain enormously by being approached by an unconventional route. For instance, the enlightened way to approach Venice is not down the motorway lined with almost as many advertisement hoardings as poplars, nor by the railway where one sees nothing until one is spewed out into a melee of hotel touts, but by an unpretentious tram from Padua which trundles pleasantly along the banks of the Brenta, past boys fishing for eels and Palladian palaces, and ends at a landing-stage, whence a ferry-boat takes one right into the city which rises miraculously out of the lagoon ahead. In the same way a driver approaching San Gimignano from Poggibonsi, as most do, should make a point of turning off the main road a few yards past Km. 8, taking an unmarked, narrow, but perfectly practicable byroad to the right. This leads straight up to the southern gate and commands an enchanting view of the brown little town and its towers across a valley of silvery olives, whereas the main road circles leftwards round a hill which blocks the view. Those who miss this view have not seen San Gimignano. [*Plate* 56.]

One comes for the towers, of course, thirteen of them today, standing square, very old, and nearly blind in the clear Tuscan sky. Once there may have been five times as many; if zealous enough in this sleepy little place, one can still trace about twenty-five truncated ones. This, on a bigger scale, is what the towers of Siena must have looked like before the Spaniards and the eighteenth-century earthquake dinged them down. In San Gimignano there was much legislation governing towers; only a noble or the owner of a merchant ship registered at Pisa might build one, and no private tower might be taller than the Torre Rognosa. The few loopholes in the stone work served only to admit some light to the stairways, while for defensive purposes each tower once ended in a sort of storks' nest or fighting-top constructed of wood. The more important families built pairs, sometimes linked at the top by wooden bridges. Although primarily built for use in private warfare, their height must owe something to the motives of pride and display, for once well above the roof-tops there cannot have been any compelling military reason to go any higher. Unless such a tower is, like a few of these, abnormally tall, it is a very solid construction—in Florence in 1944 the German demolitions near the Ponte Vecchio revealed one standing grimly up out of the ruins of the much later buildings that had surrounded and concealed it.

With its three thousand inhabitants, San Gimignano sits on a hilltop within an irregular star-shaped circuit of walls. Mercifully there are hardly any houses outside. The traveller, entering the town, perceives at once that here the architectural clock stopped some centuries before it did at Siena. One must search quite hard to find any historic building that dates from later than 1300 or thereabouts. There is more rough grey travertine and less warm brick. Walking round the streets one notices horseshoe arches in the oldest walls, which must be an import from the East via Pisa. The towers rocket up everywhere above the housetops but defy one to identify them once one has moved to the next street. The town centre—for San Gimignano, though on a very small scale, is definitely urban—has two adjoining piazzas of great character, connected at their corners like two white squares on a chess-board. This ground-plan alone ensures an interesting ensemble. In the middle of the first stands an attractive well-head of travertine bearing the ladder escutcheon of the Malavolti, one of whom was *podestà* when it was built. Beneath the piazza is a huge rainwater cistern constructed as early as 1273. In the second piazza, at the top of a broad flight of steps, is the Collegiata or collegiate church, twelfth century with a plain satisfactory façade of fifty years later. To its left stands the town hall or Palazzo del Comune of the late thirteenth century, facing the church is the older town hall or Palazzo del Podestà, obviously of great age, and to the right are the twin towers of the Salvucci family. Those of their rivals the Ardinghelli are behind the loggia, in the same block as the new town hall. [*Plates* 60, 59.]

The town arose in the twelfth century. By 1147, or probably even earlier, it had a full panoply of elected consuls, a council of fifty, and, at times of crisis, a citizens' assembly summoned by the church bell. Until 1199 it was nominally subject to the bishop of Volterra, whose two *rettori* were the judges. Then they were replaced by a *podestà*, and the bishop, in his temporal capacity at least, acquired the unpopular status of an ex-colonial power. At the same time the population had outgrown the cramped ring of the first walls, three of whose gates can be seen well within the town, and a wider second circuit was built. These are the walls that enclose the town today. From their new machicolated gateways the Sangimignanesi marched out to fight little wars against troublesome castles in their *contado* or to resist the encroachments of the episcopal colonialists from Volterra. In 1230 they cornered the warlike prelate in a castle and assailed him with 'arrows and crossbow-bolts and many stones', while he replied with the direst spiritual thunders, doubtless accompanied by some well-directed kettles of boiling oil. Villani mentions that in one such campaign in 1309 each side put seven hundred horsemen into the field. There were also the usual dissentions between *grandi* and *popolo* as well as a related conflict with the rich order of the Templars, whose commandery in the north-east corner of the town was burnt down in 1233. In the same year the guildsmen managed to get represented in the government.

At that time San Gimignano had cloth and glass-blowing industries, and pottery and tanning as well. It exported olive oil and saffron and was already noted for the white *vernaccia*, still an excellent country wine today. It had a remarkable array of social institutions, including four hospitals, a school with *un buono esperto maestro di grammatica*, an official artist (the first was Memmo, followed by his son Lippo), a bank giving credit on easy terms, public baths with hot water, a vigilance-committee of sixteen resolute men appointed to check extravagance in female fashions, and a municipal house of *donne cortesi*, whose supervisor was required to keep her establishment *ben fornita* on forty soldi a month.

The leaders of this community were as pugnacious as a pack of terriers. The troubadour Folgore had to go to Siena to sing of the gay pleasures of the different seasons; at home, as he says, 'each stirred the fire of household enmities', and nothing had precedence over the long-lasting Guelf-Ghibelline feud. This was in fact a feud between the two principal houses, the Salvucci (Ghibellines) and the Ardinghelli (Guelfs), who tirelessly revolved round each other looking for an opening. A 'binary system' like this is likely to make for as much instability in a city-state as we are told it does in the larger field of astrophysics. The hundred yards of the larger piazza was a no-man's-land between their respective pairs of towers, which must have made life difficult for everyone else. And these vendettas could be pursued without going down into the piazza. Whenever any young nobleman in his tower felt bored, he had only to send a single heavy crossbow-bolt into the top of a neighbouring tower to reproduce something like the gratifying disturbance of a red-hot volcanic pellet falling into a nest of pterodactyls.

There is an optimum size for a town as there is for any living organism, and San Gimignano was just too small to evolve socially and politically beyond the stage that Siena reached by about 1250. The town's population may have been near six thousand, with rather more than that number in its *contado*. There were not enough merchants, notaries, and weavers to impose their will and their way of life on the anarchic nobility who owned the towers. Yet on the surface at least there was plenty of constitution-mongering in this Lilliput. Everything was now a multiple of four, to correspond with the four ancient wards. There were sixty councillors, eight lords of the treasury, twelve captains and rectors of the people, sixteen good men and true to watch the *podestà*.

By bad luck the wrong faction, from the point of view of foreign policy, was often on top, so that San Gimignano's army shared in the Guelfs' defeat at Montaperti and the Ghibellines' defeat at Colle. After that the little commune became more or less a satellite of Florence and helped to take and demolish the Ghibelline stronghold of Poggibonsi, while internal matters were controlled for a time by four Captains of the Guelf Party. But this proliferation of magistrates, and even an embassy from the Guelf League headed by Dante himself, failed to reconcile the factions. Repeated disturbances were provoked by the Ardinghelli, who were as often as not in exile, and tried several times to break into the town and get even with their enemies. The strife scarcely paused for the Black Death, though the depopulated and distracted town put itself temporarily under the care of a Florentine occupying force. At last the Ardinghelli, in revenge for an unpleasant judicial murder, expelled the Salvucci with the help of most of the people. But the Florentines again occupied the place and 'pacified' it. Finally in 1353 a *parlamento* of all citizens voted for permanent and complete union with Florence. The terms were honourable, and ought to have become a model for the unification of central Italy. The Sangimignanesi were made Florentine citizens, and craftsmen among them were freely admitted to the Florentine guilds. They also kept a measure of municipal freedom and all their heraldic ceremonial, which lasted unimpaired down the centuries.

The new rulers were prompt to build a new castle within the walls. This was done, Villani assures us, 'in order to remove every cause of evil thinking from the inhabitants'. Today this Rocca, whose ruins lie behind the main church, encloses a charming garden with lemon trees and affords a good view of the towers. [*Plate* 57.]

Internal peace had not been bought at the price of life. By the time of the Renaissance, though somewhat decayed, San Gimignano had still enough taste and wealth to patronize Benedetto da Maiano, Gozzoli, and Ghirlandaio, enough sense of responsibility to be a fit audience for the first of Savonarola's ominous sermons, and enough able-bodied young men for Macchiavelli to drill outside the southern gate.

Needless to say, of all this history, the only event now clear in the minds of the inhabitants is Dante's diplomatic mission in May 1300. Until recently it featured in an annual pageant. In fact the embassy had very little importance and, in view of the poet's subsequent championship of the Ghibelline emperor against the Guelf League, was probably one which he himself preferred to forget. In case we should too, a marble tablet outside the town hall proudly proclaims the wrong date.*

San Gimignano has two saints. The one everybody knows about is Santa Fina, the little girl whose most reprehensible act before her sainthood was to accept an orange one morning down by the *fonti* from a boy who was too shy to express his feelings in any other way. She was scolded by her mother and immediately struck down by some appalling disease, which she interpreted as a penance for her sin and the world's. She was then ten years old. For the next five years she deliberately lay on a table-top on the floor instead of a bed. The paintings always show her surrounded by mice. Then, honoured by a vision of the pope, she died during a sudden whirlwind (raised by devils) while the church bells rang untouched by any hand (save those of angels, it being well known that devils do not ring bells). When they lifted her body, bits of mortified flesh remained sticking to the table. After a detail like that nothing could stop the Middle Ages from canonizing her. The only unrepellent part of the story is that every year on the day of her death (12 March) the wild wallflowers come out and splash the grey towers with yellow.

The other local saint, San Bartolo, lived at the same time. Of noble birth but a simple priest, he devoted the last twenty years of his long and useful life to caring for the lepers in their colony at Cellole; ultimately the disease blinded and killed him. His tomb in Sant' Agostino is railed off and neglected; few have heard of him.

So much for the place's history. It is worth more than a brief visit, for apart from its artistic treasures and the unique picture of an early medieval commune it gives, the

* It has just been removed at last, leaving another one inside which is rhetorically non-committal on this point.

country close around it is probably the most attractive in all Tuscany—particularly in early spring or autumn, when the pale, billowing, cypress-dotted hills are crossed by sweeps of dark brown plough. San Gimignano is ideal for a few days' stay, and although, as a local guide-book (now unfortunately out of print) says in its English version, 'there are many tourists who come here to enjoy themselves in the magnificent and suggestive view of the square and rigid towers', their orgies are circumscribed by the tight time-tables of coaches, so that the discerning visitor who puts up at the admirable *albergo* in the first square, or at some smaller hotel, will be able to explore the town undistracted in the evening or early morning. And it is at its best at sunset when, high above the travertine chasms, the screaming swifts trace lines like Simone Martini's through the cool air, or after dark, when the towers rise dramatically into the night above the pattern of lights in the piazza.

The Collegiata is one of the very few churches in Tuscany that have preserved their medieval frescoes all down the length of the aisles. On the right are the New Testament ones by Barna, done in the 1360s, full of violent action and unusually composed in some of the scenes—the *Arrest*, for instance, has a claw-shaped mass of steel helmets closing in, while the man whose ear is cut off falls backwards on his shield below, his movement completing the circular hook round the central figures. Bartolo di Fredi's Old Testament series on the other side is, though a few years later, more jumbled and naïve; we admire the frenzied Egyptians drowning in the Red Sea, the smiling camel-borne Israelite ladies in wimples, the delightful modesty of Job's wife amid the musical and culinary distractions of a medieval banquet, and the childishly thorough disaster that happens when 'Behold, there came a great wind from the wilderness, and smote the four corners of the house, and it fell upon the young men, and they are dead, and I only am escaped to tell thee.' [*Plate* 55.]

At the west end are two painted wooden statues by Jacopo della Quercia, a large *St. Sebastian* by Gozzoli, and a busy *Hell* by Taddeo di Bartolo. One should also see the Renaissance chapel of Santa Fina; its intricately contrived altar by Benedetto da Maiano matches the careful Latin of the epitaph drawing attention to Ghirlandaio's two rather stiff frescoes of her end.

They take pride and trouble in showing the Palazzo del Comune to its best advantage. From a nice little courtyard the steps lead up to the second floor, which is mostly taken up by the council chamber where Dante spoke. There are charming dark blue and ochre frescoes—hunting scenes, jousts, and Charles of Anjou receiving gifts—from as early as 1292, and an inscription urging the excitable councillors to give each speaker a fair hearing and a polite and well-reasoned answer:

Proposto:
Odi benigno ciaschun che propone,
Risponde gratioso et fa ragione.

On the longest stretch of wall Lippo Memmi has unfortunately covered these admirable

H

decorations with a *Maestà*, obviously based on the far better one which his brother-in law painted in the Siena town hall two years before. The composition lacks depth, and the phalanx of saints spreads too far laterally to be seen from across the limited width of the room. The next floor has better things to show, including a large *Virgin* by Guido da Siena, recovered a few years ago from beneath a barbarous *seicento* over-painting of all but the face, but still labelled '*ignoto Senese*'. And there are two painted crosses of the later *duecento*, one by the Florentine Coppo di Marcovaldo and the other Sienese, better spaced and more subtle in colouring, besides a well-hung collection of other works whose merits the visitor may be left to discover for himself. Finally one comes to the *camera del podestà* in the tower, frescoed with swallows, two magpies mobbing an owl, and some lively scenes of courtship and marriage. The happy couple, as surprised as we are to see them, are given a bath together in the same tub and then firmly put to bed.

The other paintings that everyone goes to see are in Sant' Agostino at the far end of the town. In a side chapel are two small frescoes by Bartolo di Fredi—one of them pleases with its impressionistic soft flurry of pink angels' wings. But the important ones are in the choir, where Benozzo Gozzoli's sharp-drawn Renaissance series tells the story of St. Augustine. So much limpid, pagan light would surely have hurt the eyes of that great but grim man. But he would have approved of Scene 1 (the bottom one on the left) where we see his first day at school, for the *Confessions*, though liberal enough to admit that corporal punishment is a hindrance to learning, tell us that at least it stops the young from being too cheerful. Gozzoli's next pictures do not hint at the wild oats Augustine sowed while up at the university, or at the heresies which worried his mother so much more. As is well known, St. Monica was one of those mothers, and what she feared for her darling boy was not damp socks or even mistresses, but the hell-fire that waits for those with the wrong opinions. The distraught woman besieged heaven with her prayers (Scene 3) and pestered every bishop she met, until one of them, poor man, assured her that 'the child of so many tears could not be eternally lost'. Augustine, whose mature judgement would have rejected this view, tried to get some peace by sailing to Rome without telling her beforehand (Scene 4). After lecturing there (Scene 6, and Gozzoli is getting bored) he moved to Milan (Scene 7, with its gay cavalcade through the Roman Campagna, was what Gozzoli liked doing and is much better). There he encountered the robust faith of its bishop, St. Ambrose, and a newly published imperial edict establishing that faith as the official religion (Scene 8). To these persuasions were added the entreaties of St. Monica, who had caught up with him and had to be introduced to St. Ambrose (Scene 9). Augustine's conscience was just beginning to develop into the alarming organ it became in later life; the unfortunate woman who had been his faithful companion for ten years was abruptly banished to Africa, leaving their son with him; and Augustine, entangled simultaneously with another lady and with anxious theological issues, offered up for the last time his well-known prayer to be granted the great gift of chastity—'only not yet'. Scene 10 does scant justice to the last inner crisis in the garden which brought these vacillations to an end. His inevitable baptism by St.

Ambrose follows in Scene 11, in which Gozzoli has inserted some words from the *Te Deum* to remind us that the two saints are said to have composed it together, for St. Ambrose, as Gibbon observes, 'prudently introduced into the church of Milan the useful institution of a loud and regular psalmody'. [*Plate* 58.]

The rest of Augustine's life is more briefly indicated on the same lines in the topmost frescoes, which have been damaged in patches and are anyway too high to see. Among the heretics he refutes are doubtless the followers of that misguided fifth-century Welshman Morgan or Pelagius, who capped his many errors by denying that babies are punished eternally if they die before they are baptized. Augustine, a strict but humane thinker, held that their physical torments are slight.

Gozzoli's anecdotes make no more effort to come to grips with the deeper side of Augustine than do the preceding paragraphs. Nothing in these pictures suggests his stature as a writer, the stern theology that at second hand moulded Scotland over a thousand years afterwards, or his tremendous concept, amid so much nonsense, of the City of God surviving the crash of Rome. Clearly Gozzoli, the fashionable painter whose aim is to show forth the pride of life, finds the saint's values so impossible that he does not even indicate the more serious predicaments of the human being. Augustine's emotional life-span in a shipwrecked age is shown as a clever prelate's smooth career. The painting is more solid than in Pinturicchio's series on Æneas Sylvius, but the treatment is shallower biographically, and with less justification.

The best thing is to forget about Augustine and look at these pictures for their own sake, for the best of them are bright with the fresh light of the early Renaissance. There is a tremendous wealth of architecture in some of the backgrounds, and perhaps a good deal of symbolism. Why, for instance, does he insert tie-rods so lavishly to hold the loggia at Milan together? Is it because it is a pagan structure, and therefore already unsafe?

Several small churches have frescoes too—San Pietro, the Templars' church (but the view outside the gate is better), and San Lorenzo in Ponte. The guide-book already mentioned describes the damaged wall-paintings in this last church in words which deserve to be quoted, if only to preserve in print the extraordinary patter of an English-speaking guide in an Italian church:

> 'Stories of S. Benedetto divided in 7 compartments of which only two are in fairly good conditions and they represent: The miracle of a broken plate re-fixed entirely, and the consecration of a new priest, on top the death of S.B. On the front* Paradise but the frescoe is partly spoiled. Below S. Michel weighing the Souls, and St. Peter who bless and direct same to the entrance of Paradise, above Saints hosannating. . . . The Hell of popular or Gregorian conception. It is worth noted the group of Clergymen.'

On this happily anti-clerical note we may end our survey of San Gimignano, a most

* I.e. opposite, *di fronte*.

delightful place, though not without mentioning how friendly the people are, and what trouble they will take if one shows an interest in their town. But before leaving the neighbourhood no one should forget to go out to the little Romanesque church of Cellole, two or three miles to the north-west on a hill among cypresses. It is one of the most charming and perfect small churches of its kind in the whole region.

12

Four Hill Towns

THE DRIVE TO Massa Marittima takes one forty miles through the Colline Metallifere, interesting wooded country verging on the mountainous. The way leads close past San Galgano. This great Cistercian abbey, now in ruins, was one of the first purely Gothic buildings in central Italy and dates from 1224 or earlier. It is dedicated to a local saint, a knight who became a hermit when his sword stuck fast in a crevice of rock. The chaste piers and arches built by French monks look oddly out of place so far south, and the abbey is more of a curiosity to Italians than it is to us. In fact the style was imported into Italy ready-made, spreading northwards from the Cistercian abbeys of Fossanova and Casamari down beyond Rome. Among several purely French features is the way in which the half-columns on the piers of the nave are corbelled off well before they reach the ground.

In its time San Galgano was one of the leading religious houses of the whole area, and supplied Siena with architects and city treasurers. At the end of the Middle Ages it declined, Sir John Hawkwood plundered it, and in 1397 the unfortunate abbot of the day was left the sole inmate. The abbey recovered in the next century, but a Renaissance pope outdid Hawkwood by making over its entire income to one of his more expensively living cardinals. In due course the monks left and, after a further interval, the building was deconsecrated, though not before the small congregation of peasants had nearly been killed when the tower collapsed during Mass. The Church could destroy an abbey just as effectively as any royal heretic.

After San Galgano comes a region of large villages, each set on a hill nearly two thousand feet high and approached by abrupt unfenced corkscrew turns which the enormous buses take happily in their stride. No traffic authority at home would license the route, which diverges from the more sedate main road in several places, but it must be admitted that Italian bus drivers do this sort of thing extremely well.

Massa, on its inevitable hilltop, has a distant and limited view of the sea. In the other direction, across a fertile valley where the lines of olive trees make an attractive diagonal pattern against the strips of red plough, the wooded hills rise to the horizontal straggle of a mining village and a long crag on the skyline. In spring, on a day when cloud-shadows and patches of sunlight chase each other across the landscape, it bears a curious resemblance to Wales.

Almost everything worth seeing is concentrated round the triangular piazza, which, incidentally, would look better if it were not used as an inadequate car-park. Here is the Romanesque cathedral, raised on a stepped plinth higher than Siena's and with a very fine tower of the same period, as well as the two town halls. All are in travertine, the *palazzi* silvery grey and the cathedral a warmer shade. The latter was started in 1228, probably by one Enrico da Campione. The west end facing the piazza has a simple Pisan-type façade with three tiers of blind arches resting on columns; the lowest tier of tall engaged columns is carried round the flanks of the church and makes a very satisfactory decoration. If Giovanni Pisano had any part in it, as is claimed, it was only in finishing the topmost section of the west front, for most of the sculptures are in an older style than his. The transepts, apse, and brick cupola were added later, at intervals, and the inside is disappointing architecturally. [*Plate* 61.]

Both the Palazzo Comunale, which incorporates an earlier tower, and the smaller Palazzo del Podestà with its many coats of arms of vanished dignitaries, have windows of a pattern different from those of Sienese palaces, the heads being round instead of pointed. This local variation has been copied in such old or would-be-old buildings as the town can boast.

The larger of the two civic palaces contains one of the three pictures that must be seen in Massa. For Massa's works of art are few but good. This one is a small *Maestà* by Ambrogio Lorenzetti, all gilding and bright colours. The picture, a late work of his, is very strongly constructed and alive with light and energy, though the central figure appears rather flat and unattractive compared with the busily fiddling angels and peculiar conjuring Virtues in the foreground. The second picture of merit is a sad, graceful *Virgin* in the north transept of the cathedral, probably by Segna di Bonaventura, a larger panel than most and an impressive work. The third and last is a group of scenes from the Passion, now in the crypt. They are obviously derived from Duccio's *Maestà*, but opinions differ as to which of his close followers painted them. Apparently it was not Segna.

The sculptures are even better. The earliest and to the non-specialist eye the most delightful are the blackened eleventh-century carvings in the north-west corner of the cathedral. There is much variety, for instance a delicate little Virgin within a *mandorla* with four angels, and on a larger and cruder scale the Twelve Apostles in a row, clasping books with the happy, loopy expression of children at a rural school-treat. Their robes are most vigorously stylized, the swing of the folds making a nice contrast with faces that have been scrubbed and placated into total rigidity. Next in order of time come the Pisan-style *duecento* carvings outside the cathedral, most of them on the façade, where some really splendid demi-lions jut out above the lowest capitals, mangling their prey. The architrave over the door, which looks badly in need of restoration, tells the story of St. Cerbonius, bishop of a more rustic Massa in the Dark Ages, who when summoned to Rome milked wild animals on the way and drove a flock of geese before him as a present for the pope. On receiving the pontifical blessing the birds were apparently all inspired to fly home again, rather than wait for Michaelmas. St. Cerbonius also appears with his geese on a panel of the very fine font of 1267 by Giroldo da Como; the other three sides tell the life of John the Baptist. Lastly, in the crypt, is the saint's memorial sarcophagus carved in 1324 by Goro di Gregorio from Siena, in whose pale marble the legend is presented once again with Gothic charm and grace.

This sequence of carvings, from which one can learn a great deal about the development of this art over three crucial centuries, practically brings to an end the short list of things that must be seen in Massa. There are other churches, but some are uninteresting and others are shut because their foundations are unsafe. There is nothing out of the ordinary, by Tuscan standards, in the streets of the town, only many steep wynds and dark entrances, some crumbling ramparts and gates, and a battered little stone *palazzetto* that once housed the mint. Rather unusually, this lower part round the main piazza and cathedral is the older part, the Città Vecchia, corresponding to the original free commune which flourished in the thirteenth century, thanks to the copper and silver mines nearby. (Massa boasts the oldest Mining Statute in Italy.) When the Sienese took over in 1337 they engaged the architect Agnolo di Ventura to build more impressive fortifications on the hill above, surrounding a Città Nuova. This part of the town is approached up a very steep lane and through the big embattled Porta alle Silici, which is linked with the pre-existing castle of the old commune, now called the Torre dell' Orologio, by a wide arch flung boldly across the intervening space. Beyond this point there is little need to go, unless one is so indefatigable as to look for San Bernardino's birthplace.

Massa has a less stormy history than most of these towns. It seems to have accepted Sienese control more or less unemotionally, and almost died of malaria and neglect after the coming of the Medici Grand Dukes. Even today it is a backwater, and a shameful peace, from the Italian standpoint, descends on the main street well before midnight.

Montalcino, twenty-five miles south of Siena, is the homely hill town to which Montluc's force and the Sienese government in exile, with something like two thousand of its citizens, retired after Siena fell to the Spaniards in 1555. The steepness and height of the hill, rising to 1,850 feet straight out of the plain, is a measure of their desperate situation. The townsfolk, who had successfully resisted the same enemy two years earlier and whose fathers had lived under unbroken Sienese rule since 1260, gave their unswerving support to the exiled leaders. The Republic was re-established in its new capital and coins were struck bearing the she-wolf and the words: *Libertas: Resp. Senens in M. Ilcino*. Like most governments in exile, however, this one had its troubles with its foreign protectors. M. de Soubise, who replaced Montluc, was considered overbearing in his manner. Luckily the Sienese authorities were able to petition for Montluc's recall. Our Gascon hero returned, and the alliance was once more cordial. He would not discuss M. de Soubise, either at the time or afterwards in his book. Instead he gave himself to restoring morale and defending Montalcino.

First he discovered a plot within the fortress headed by a Calabrian soldier of fortune whom the Spanish commander, Don García de Toledo, had bribed. Then, rightly believing that in such a situation attack is the best defence, he led out a number of energetic sorties, cleared the enemy away from the immediate neighbourhood, and once very nearly took Don García prisoner. After this revival they took their alliance with France very seriously in Montalcino. When Mary Tudor lost Calais, they rang their bells for three days without a break. In dark days a Stalingrad, however remote, is worth celebrating.

After four years came the fatal treaty of Cateau-Cambrésis, one of whose clauses decreed that the French should withdraw from their last outpost in Italy. With Montluc and his troops gone, further resistance against the Habsburg–Medici combine was out of the question, and on 31 July 1559 Montalcino ceased to be a sovereign state. In these circumstances it is remarkable, and a great tribute to the personalities concerned, that the French left so good a name behind them. When Montaigne visited the place some years later, he found that 'the memory of the French is maintained in such great affection that you can scarce remind the people of it without tears coming into their eyes'.

Today Montalcino has its history, its market, its castle (in which is kept the standard that Sodoma designed for the exiles), several disproportionately large churches standing up on the skyline, and a tremendous view towards all points except due south. There is also a simple, old-fashioned inn, where the food is good and one spends most of one's time in the kitchen watching it being cooked.

The Palazzo Pubblico is frankly rustic. Sant' Agostino has some frescoes, of which the most entertaining are those of the life of St. Anthony the Abbot, with squat Stanley Spencerish hermits in dressing-gowns. Given the general roughstone appearance of Montalcino, it is a surprise to find two beautifully arranged little art galleries, one civic and the other in the seminary next Sant' Agostino. The latter has such things as a *Madonna of the Cherries* by Pietro Lorenzetti, a Segna polyptych, an early Sodoma and one of those painted crosses of Umbrian pattern which mark the beginnings of medieval painting in this region. There is also a collection of painted wooden statues; the two least devotional ones, by a late follower of the Maitani, are a real delight to the eye.

The Museo Civico, at the northern end of the town, is better labelled and needs even less introduction. Here the most attractive exhibit is a little masterpiece by Sano di Pietro, worthy of Sassetta, which should be better known to Sano's many modern detractors.

Six miles along a quiet country road winding southwards through the hills brings one to the largest and by far the noblest Romanesque church in the whole of the Sienese *contado*. No one, however pressed for time or tired of churches, should miss Sant' Ántimo. Here it stands in a gentle valley among olive trees, between which the spring and autumn ploughing turns up brilliant red strips of earth. The abbey is lonely and disused, yet roofed and perfect but for the porch some peasants demolished to make more room for their carts to pass. Being well off the beaten track, it is not much visited, and the custodian has usually to be fetched from the hilltop village a mile away. [*Plate* 63.]

Sant' Antimo was founded by Charlemagne's son, and the present sacristy with its rude apse and the tiny crypt below represent the church he built, as old as any in Sienese territory. The main abbey building dates from about 1100; there is a long inscription by a donor dated 1118, which starts on the altar steps and runs on to a nearby pillar. The script should interest palaeographers. The Benedictine monks used a beautiful stone which is still quarried near the village, a hard travertine with translucent veins of pale golden alabaster. They carved superb capitals in this material, one in particular showing Daniel among the lions, but the greatest beauty of this church lies in its bold, simple architecture. The main feature is that the aisles continue round the east end to form a semicircular ambulatory of the same width, with three small apsidal chapels. There is also a large triforium gallery. This plan, seldom found in Italy but common in parts of France, was based on that of the great Benedictine abbey of Cluny, rebuilt a few years before. At all events this church, like the Gothic San Galgano, looks French rather than central Italian. Some of the carvings from the destroyed west porch have been preserved. They are less subtle than the capitals and are nearly two centuries later. Altogether, and not least for its situation, Sant' Antimo is unforgettable.

From Montalcino the road leads down to San Quirico, a particularly dull walled townlet on the Via Francigena, where the men in hats do not even stand upright in the small piazza to conduct their interminable bargains and discussions, but lean listlessly against the walls. One stops briefly to see the twelfth-century church with three sculpture-laden doors. The oldest of them is flanked by groups of four columns, standing on lions' backs and reef-knotted half-way up, while Romanesque crocodiles snap at each other on the lintel. Beyond San Quirico the road to Rome crosses the bleak clay basin well described in Contessa Origo's *War in Val d'Órcia*. Away to the right, beyond the ruined castle of Rocca d'Orcia which stands up on the foothills and which, when owned by the Salimbeni, was a continual menace to the peace of the district, the gentle volcanic cone of Monte Amiata rises to 5,650 feet, by far the highest mountain between Florence and Rome. It is rich in unusual minerals, including mercury and the earth from which the famous pigment of Siena, raw or burnt, has hitherto been made. Now the latter workings are being closed as uneconomic and a chemical substitute will find its way on to artists' palettes. [*Plate* 62.]

Two years before he died, our friend Æneas Sylvius returned to the district he had known and loved as a boy, establishing himself with the whole Vatican apparatus on the slopes of Monte Amiata and making the abbey of San Salvatore his headquarters. Here he passed the summer months while his architect put the finishing touches to the buildings that were to transform the pope's birthplace on the other side of the Val d'Orcia. There was no point in going to see them before they were ready. Book IX of the *Commentaries* opens with a description of this prolonged pontifical picnic.

> '. . . And on certain days they all attended the *segnatura*, which the Pontiff held in the woods, sometimes under one tree and sometimes under another, but never far from the gentle murmur of running water. He changed the place each time, always finding some new spring in a dell or some fresh patch of shade, in fact so many that it was hard to choose. It happened one day when the Pontiff was signing some document that a pack

of hounds tracked down a huge stag which had been lying close by all the time. The beast, using its hooves and horns, scattered them and went bounding off to higher ground. And from time to time he would hold a consistory with the cardinals beneath the chestnuts and receive embassies in the meadows. Every day the Pontiff went riding through the forests accompanied by officials of the Curia, and transacted confidential and public business with them as they went along. At sunset he used to go out a short way beyond the monastery, to a place where one could look down on the valley of the Paglia, and there he would sit with the monks enjoying their conversation. How wonderfully peaceful it was.'

Mira suavitas! His only disappointment was that the cherries had not yet ripened. But there was time for that. News filtered through of fresh crises in the everlasting power-politics of Central Europe, but from the chestnut woods of Amiata these things could be seen in their proper perspective. People coming up from the valley reported that it was like a furnace. Presently it got cooler, but life was very pleasant in these highlands and the air was good for the pope's fast failing health. What with one thing and another, the picnic-party did not return to Rome until mid-December.

The road to Rome, which we were following, climbs up out of the Val d'Orcia and over a boulder-strewn moor until it reaches the Sienese and Tuscan border at Radicófani. Here on a basalt plug, set high above a windswept pass with a tremendous view, stands the ruined castle once held by a colourful character named Ghino di Tacco, the Robin Hood of Italy. How he restored to health a self-indulgent abbot, whom he kidnapped and kept on a sensible diet, makes one of the few stories in the *Decameron* which are suitable for family reading. After Ghino's time the castle was less helpfully garrisoned by the frontier troops of the Sienese Republic and the Grand Duchy, until it was blown up by accident in the feckless eighteenth century. Many generations of indomitable British travellers have passed this way in the days when this road was the chief route to Rome, and, until the age of our grandfathers, have braced themselves with whatever the inn could offer before confronting the rumoured enormities of the Papal States. Their reactions to Radicofani itself have seldom varied since the entry in *Evelyn's Diary* for 2 November 1644:

> 'On the sum'it of this horrid rock (for so it is) is built a very strong fort, garrison'd, and somewhat beneath it is a small towne; the provisions are drawne up with ropes and engines, the precipice being otherwise inaccessable. At one end of the towne lie heapes of rocks so strangely broaken off from the ragged mountaine as would affright one with their horror and menacing postures. Just opposite to the inn gushed out a plentiful and most useful fountaine which falls into a great trough of stone, bearing the Duke of Tuscany's armes.'

Those whose taste is classical rather than romantic should have turned off to the left at San Quirico and gone up to Pienza. Until 1459 this place was the quite undistinguished village of Corsignano, graced only by its Romanesque church, which can still be found on a delightful hillside among cypresses, chestnuts, and olives, half a mile outside the walls—it has a round tower, mermaids and knights on its two door-lintels, and the venerable font in which the future pope was baptized. Then Pius II, stopping on his way to the great conference where he meant to harness Europe's every effort to the crusade, decided to convert Corsignano into Pienza. Happy inconsistency! Bernardo Rossellino was engaged to create the nucleus of the new town and was allocated 18,000 ducats with which to do it. Working at top speed and using for the most part the easily cut *tufo*, he finished the task in three years, with some help from Alberti. For the Piccolomini palace here, as in his other one at Siena, he kept close to the Florentine models, except that on the south side, facing the small formal garden and the drop to the open valley beyond, he placed three loggias along the length of the building, one above the other, thus opening it up magnificently and satisfying his patron's requirement, too seldom made in Italy, that 'the first adornment of a palace should be light'. [*Pls.* 64, 65.]

For the cathedral, for Pienza was to become a see, the pope had his own ideas. His *Wanderjahre* in southern Germany had shown him, at Nuremberg, Vienna, and elsewhere, a type of church known as a *Hallenkirche*, an arrangement combining late Gothic lines with the maximum of light, the aisles being as high as the nave and a *chevet* of chapels radiating round the high altar. To this basic plan Rossellino was allowed to add Italian decorated vaulting and a façade of his own excellent Renaissance design. The windows are Gothic. Only an architect of genius could have made a success of such a hybrid, as most people will agree that Rossellino did.

The site being cramped, he had to splay the lines of the piazza and build the east (or really the south) end of the church right on the edge of the precipice. The foundations rest on solid sandstone, but forty feet down this changes to clay with porous layers. A crack appeared even before the church was finished, and Rossellino himself was not too happy about it. 'Time will tell,' said his imperturbable employer. After five centuries the choir of the cathedral has sunk by several feet and tilted outwards through an appreciable angle; presently it can hardly fail to collapse altogether, unless gigantic injections of concrete deep underground can restore stability. Meanwhile the glass indicators recently fixed across the cracks continue to split almost from one year to the next. [*Plates* 66, 67.]

If nature now threatens this building, Pius, doubtless foreseeing the Baroque period, saw to it that man should not. While still in Pienza for the opening celebrations he published a bull excommunicating anyone who should presume to alter any part of it.

Several pictures were specially commissioned for the interior from Sienese artists of the day. The result, as usually happens, was mixed. They all look well from a distance with their golden backgrounds and in their Renaissance frames. Closer inspection reveals, first, a Sano di Pietro whose central figure is better than the rest of it. Next, probably the best picture Vecchietta painted, an *Assumption* in which the Virgin is borne aloft by bevies of flouncy musical angels, the frail beardless pope on the left being a likeness of Pius II. Last comes a frightful Matteo di Giovanni which plumbs depths of affectation rare in Sienese art, even of this period. Better than any of these are Rossellino's own little carved altar for St. Andrew's chapel and his font in the crypt or baptistery below. [*Plate* 35.]

The Piccolomini palace may be visited. After walking through the faded glories of the papal apartments, one emerges on to the loggia, and sees what delighted Pius five hundred years ago and made him forgive Rossellino for having exceeded his estimate of the cost by nearly three times as much.

> 'From the three porticoes which face the sun at mid-day the view extends to Amiata, that towering and densely wooded mountain which We have described. Thence the eye travels down into the Val d'Orcia, passing over green pasture-lands and hills clothed with long grass or rich corn in season, and many vineyards, and so up again to castles and villages set on precipitous rocks, and to the right as far as a place called Bagno di Vignoni, and leftwards to Monte Cetona, which is higher than Radicofani and is the portal of the winter sun.'

A pleasant town-hall-cum-loggia was added at the back of the piazza, completing Rossellino's task and the buildings paid for out of the papal exchequer. The cardinals, who were now expected to build themselves suitable palaces at their own expense, were faced with a delicate problem. None of them shared their master's enthusiasm for country life in southern Tuscany, nor was the papal court at all likely to stay in this outlandish place after he had gone. Yet to disobey might be unwise. The most ambitious of them, Cardinal Borgia, acquired the remaining building on the piazza and, by adding a few Renaissance touches and another storey, judiciously converted it into an adequate stepping-stone to promotion. His economy is still apparent if one runs one's eye over the masonry of what is now the bishop's palace. On the other hand, his début into the social life of the neighbourhood was less cautious. With considerable but in his case surely foreseeable skill, the future Alexander VI so arranged the evening that all the ladies of Siena found themselves being entertained on a generous scale away from their own menfolk, who were somehow excluded from that part of the party. Next morning the startled pontiff dictated a note in his stiffest Latin. 'The dancing, We are informed, was thoroughly licentious, no incitements to debauchery being spared. . . . Can it become your station to wanton with young girls and to pelt them with fruit?' But the Renaissance had got the bit between its teeth, and the good Pius was alone with the Sienese husbands in thinking the episode odd.

The little museum on the other side of the cathedral has one really remarkable thing to show, a thirteenth-century embroidered cope of English workmanship, a gift to Pius from Byzantium, where they added a border to it. And if time allows one might see the Spedaletto, down in the Orcia valley four or five miles away. It is an early fifteenth-century fortified grange, once belonging to the Hospital at Siena, and the best example of several of its kind in the district.

During the final struggles of the Sienese Republic at Montalcino, Pienza changed hands several times. The great Montluc has left us a spirited account of how he made a night-attack on the place in order to rescue some prisoners. He must be allowed to tell the story in his own words.

> *'Il y avoit un trou à la muraille, du costé de la où ie devois venir de Montalsin, qui estoit par là où sortoient les immondicitez de la ville, & par cest endroit là il y avoit deux murailles, celle de dehors estoit hors d'eschelle, & celle de dedans de quatorze ou quinze degrez. . . . Par ce trou, il falloit passer le ventre à terre, & dans l'ordure, & on se trouvoit entre deux murailles. J'avois fait faire une petite eschelle de la hauteur qu'il falloit: mais elle estoit foible, & deliée: afin qu'elle peust passer par ce trou: de sorte que malaisément un homme se pouvoit tenir dessus. . . . Je baillay la charge de porter l'eschelle aux gentilshommes, qui estoient de ma suite . . . & les priay d'entrer par le trou. . . .*
>
> *'Et de prime arrivée nous fut tiré une grãde salve d'arquebuziers, mais pour cela nous nous n'arrestasmes. . . . Tous entrèrent par dedans iceluy l'un apres l'autre. Et comme ils eurent dressé l'eschelle à la petite muraille, pour entrer dans la ville, les Gentils-hommes miens montèrent, & de dessus la muraille en hors se jettent sur un fumier. Et comme le capitaine Faustin & ses vingt hommes virent les nostres dedans, ils se voulurent haster de monter & chargèrent tant l'eschelle qu'elle rompist. Souvent ces ardeurs inconsiderées perdent les enterprises. . . . Ils furent contraincts de sortir par le mesme trou. Et me vint dire le capitaine Faustion la mal-fortune de tous mes gens, & me voyla en désespoir, voyant que pour penser recouvrer ceux qui estoient prisonniers dans la ville, j'avois esté si mal-heureux de perdre tous les Gentils-hommes de ma suite.'*

It was already daylight, an attack on another section of the walls had also failed, and the expected reinforcements had not arrived. But in the margin we read the comforting words, *Un chef peut presque tout.*

> *'J'assemblay tous les capitaines. . . . Et là je commençay à leur remonstrer, que je n'estois pas venu que pour prendre la ville. . . . Allons donc mes amis, leur dis-je, suyvez vostre Capitaine, & vous verrez, que nous aurons d'honneur. Lors je baissois la teste, ayant l'espée en la main et mon page qui portoit mon halebarde aupres de moy, tirant droit à la porte. J'avois douze Suisses de ma garde qui me suivirent, aussi fit tout le reste. . . .'*

The gate had been walled up carelessly with bricks of bad quality, and its arch gave cover to Montluc's small party.

> *'Les ennemis, qui estoient sur la porte, tiroient à grands coups de pierres sur nos gens. Les Suisses avecques leurs halebardes faisoient leur devoir contre ceste muraille de bricque. J'avois l'espée à la main gauche, & la dague à le droite: & avecques la dague je brisois & coupois la brique. Et comme nous eusmes fait un trou, dans lequel je pouvois mettre le bras, . . . je tiray à moy la muraille de telle roideur que tout le dessus d'icelle tomba sur moy, & me couvrit tout, de maniere qu'il fallust que le capitaine de ma garde me tirast de desoubs la brique, & me relevast. Et tout incontinent avecques les allebardes achevasmes de la mettre par terre.*

> *'Les deux eschelles se touchoient. Je commençay à crier à ceux qui estoient dessus l'autre, & les pousser, leur disant, sautez soldats, je me jetteray apres vous dedans. . . . Et alors je sautay à terre de nostre costé, & recommençay à crier, poussez capitaines, poussez capitaines, nous sommes dedans. . . . Et voilà le delivrance heureuse.'* *

The town was taken, the prisoners freed, and three enemy colours borne back in triumph to Montalcino.

From Pienza to Montepulciano, unless one is in a hurry, one should take the byroad through Monticchiello rather than the main road which runs further north. Starting at an easily missed turning downhill, just outside the south-east gate, one is soon passing along a narrow neck between wrinkled grey-blue precipices, through a particularly fantastic patch of *creta* where the peasants, with a pertinacity worthy of the Dutch, have somehow managed to grow corn on the confusion of hummocks above the crumbling clay gulleys. Leaving this Giovanni di Paolo landscape behind, the road goes down into a valley and up again to Monticchiello, a clean friendly little village inside medieval walls. Here one can stop to admire the Sienese arms above the gate, a Pietro Lorenzetti and some curious frescoes in the church, and a stouthearted record in the wars, for Monticchiello scored points off fifteenth-century bandits, the Spaniards both before and after the siege of Siena, and the fascist militia in 1944.

Montepulciano, when one gets there, is the largest and the highest of these hill-towns south of Siena, 605 metres or just short of 2,000 feet. It climbs up its steep ridge like an Italian Stirling, having one long main street and various ramifications, especially towards the top. Too small to develop successfully as an independent commune, Montepulciano passed several unhappy centuries as a bone of contention between Siena and Florence, with frequent changes of alliance and overlord and occasional interventions from Orvieto and Perugia. From the time of Montaperti onwards it was more often than not under some sort of Sienese control, while its kaleidoscopic politics were bedevilled by the ambitions and treacheries of the Pécora family. When Siena's power faltered at the end of the *trecento*, at the time of the Visconti domination, Montepulciano revolted and transferred its loyalty to Florence. A hundred years later it returned briefly to Siena once more, but in 1511 that enlightened dictator Pandolfo Petrucci finally gave up a colony that was not worth the trouble it took to hold. From then on the town was ruled effectively by Florence and shared in the economic and artistic expansion of the later Florentine Renaissance. It had already given to the Medici court its leading humanist scholar, Politian or Poliziano. The town from which he took his name was raised to the status of a city and was almost entirely rebuilt by Florentine architects, while two more of its sons attained fame as Pope Marcellus II and Cardinal Bellarmine.

This is therefore a town of the *cinquecento*, some sixty or seventy years later than Pienza. To go from the one to the other is an architectural experience not to be missed. It is fascinating to see how the best Italian taste developed as the Renaissance drew on towards its close. Montepulciano is a town of doorways with heavily rusticated vous-

* Montluc, *Commentaires*, Livre IV, pp. 584 ff.

soirs round the arches—long-and-short, or stepped, or flowing sideways into larger masses of rustication. Pediments appear above the more important windows, balustrades and friezes are added, the proportions have been re-designed and are usually quite excellent. In short the later Classical style is there in all its self-assurance, and it is very hard to say what exactly has been lost in the process, though some subtle quality that was present in the Piccolomini palaces has gone.

We owe this transformation, in the first place, to Antonio da Sangallo the Elder. In the year that the Florentines took over, 1511, they sent him here to modernize the ramparts. His reconstruction of the main gate at the bottom of the town so impressed the council that they granted him citizen rights and even a patent of nobility. Thus encouraged, he stayed on to build the honey-coloured church of San Biagio half-way down the olive-covered slope outside the walls. Inspired by Bramante's original plan for St. Peter's in Rome, Sangallo built his temple in the form of a Greek cross, tall, with four equal arms and a central dome, to which a lower semi-circular sacristy and a campanile were added. Two towers were envisaged but only one was actually built. Though an early example of one of those towers which the Renaissance delighted to decorate learnedly with columns of the different orders, one cannot help regretting that it was allowed to spoil the church's symmetry. The interior is a masterpiece of proportion. The decorative rosettes may be a little too heavy and too uniform, but the building as Sangallo left it is very near indeed to perfection, and a wonderful thing to find standing out here in the Italian countryside. Unhappily the ecclesiastical authorities, from the Counter-Reformation on, frowned on Greek crosses and never rested until one of the arms had been decorated almost out of recognition, first by an altar which was designed by Sangallo but finished fussily some sixty years later, and then by a local painter who did his worst on the vault above it. But with one's back to all this, one can still admire the interior as this great architect meant it to be seen, an expression of truth in stone.*

At the same time the leading families clamoured to have their *palazzi* rebuilt by him. Vignola and the younger Sangallo were called in to help complete what the elder had begun. As a result no two authorities agree about who designed and who built what. Most of them come down in favour of Sangallo the Elder as the creator of the Cervini Contacci, and Pecora palaces, and in Vignola's favour as regards those of the Tarugi and Avignonesi. It does not matter much, for they are all works of the same school. [*Pl.* 70.]

Inside the main gate is the *Marzocco*, the Florentine lion on a pillar which replaced a Sienese she-wolf. Next it stands the Palazzo Avignonesi, with two lions' heads projecting from the stonework. A few yards further up, on the same side, is the Palazzo Bucelli, its lowest courses composed of an intriguing jumble of Roman and Etruscan fragments. Almost opposite is the Palazzo Paolini (or Pecora or even Cocconi, for some of these palaces change their names often). Further on the clock tower has a figure of Punchinello to strike the hours, facing Michelozzo's façade for the dull church of Sant' Agostino. Next come an archway and a loggia and presently, on the left, the Palazzo

* There is a church of the same period, not unlike it, at Todi in Umbria.

Cervini, one of the best; it is set round three sides of a small courtyard, with cleverly graded masonry, alternate triangular and curved pediments over the windows, and a tablet to the memory of Garibaldi. Then the Gesù church, a restrained Baroque interior worth a glance.

If in need of a break from architecture at this point, one can turn aside to look for the ox-carts. Just before Politian's modest house, a turning to the left leads down to one of the town gates, and here is a blacksmith's forge to which the peasants bring ploughs and other gear to be repaired. Their carts stand outside the gate while they unload and begin eloquent explanations in the shade of the arch. They are delightful bright red carts, peculiar to the district, with painted decorations and curious struts curving above the yoke-pole, and sometimes the oxen are of the true Maremma breed, with majestic horns.

At the end of the main street is a church containing a small picture of Duccio's school, whence a turning up to the right brings one past Cardinal Bellarmine's house and into the main piazza—a large square situated so far up at the top of the town that the motor age has blessedly left it almost empty.

There is not much to be said for the cathedral, rebuilt from 1570 onwards by Ammannati and Scalza, and still lacking a façade. It contains a huge altarpiece by Taddeo di Bartolo, a little Sano di Pietro placed on one of the left-hand piers, a Della Robbia and two grotesque early statues, and some scattered fragments of sculpture set into walls and pillars and belonging to the dismantled tomb of a local man of letters, Bartolommeo Aragazzi. This worthy made his fortune as secretary to Pope Martin V and insisted on ordering for himself a disproportionately grandiose tomb by Michelozzo. As a counter-measure, one of his literary rivals wrote a catty article describing an encounter with an over-strained team of oxen and a blaspheming carter, engaged in dragging the lumps of uncut marble up the hill.

The town hall looks Florentine, and not a distinguished example of the type. It is the Palazzo Tarugi that makes the square, a dignified late Renaissance building of most original design, with engaged Ionic columns, two loggias (the upper one unfortunately walled up at some later time), and none of those fussy tricks of rustication. There is a fine well-head next it, with the Medici arms balanced by lions upon the cross-beam. A few doors down the Via Ricci is Peruzzi's simple palace of the same name, and nearly opposite, the Palazzo Bombagli, a last example of Sienese Gothic and now the museum. It should be visited, if for nothing else, for the well-known and delightfully convincing picture of St. Francis by his near-contemporary Margaritone da Arezzo, a slight, full-length, big-eyed figure in a huge cowl. Of the half-dozen versions of this picture scattered about central Italy, this one is probably the best. There is also an 'excavated' painting by a close follower of Duccio, whom Professor Carli identifies as the Master of La Grotta, and a surprising collection of works from other schools and countries, of which a Rembrandt, a Vandyke, a Velazquez, and a Giorgione are perhaps the most memorable.

For those who have seen enough *cinquecento* buildings for one day, and may even feel that the writer has not kept his promise to deal out pictures to them sparingly, there is the view. From any vantage-point on the edge of the town, the eye is caught by fresh enchanting permutations of sunlight, olive, vine, cypress, and shapely hill. And eastwards, on a clear day, the prospect is immense. It extends over the broad Val di Chiana, across Lake Trasimene and its companions, as far as Umbria and the Apennines, and so out of a region to whose unique blend of landscape, history, and art this book is an affectionate and most inadequate tribute. [*Plates* 68, 69.]

A Note on Books

THERE ARE NO books in English on the history of Siena more recent than

Douglas, L. *A History of Siena* (John Murray, 1902).
Gardner, E. *The Story of Siena and San Gimignano* (Dent, 1902).
Schevill, F. *Siena* (Chapman and Hall, 1909).

Of these three histories, *Douglas* is the fullest and has interesting if occasionally dated chapters on architecture and the arts, *Gardner* is the most detailed topographically, and *Schevill* is the best for the commune's political development.

An introduction to medieval towns in general, with some interesting remarks on Siena, is

Clark, Miss M. V. *The Medieval City State* (Methuen, 1926).

Much has been written on the Sienese painters, some of it technical and some of it partly out of date. The most recent and authoritative treatment, in large format with many reproductions in colour, is

Carli, E. *Sienese Painting* (New York Graphic Society, 1956).

This should be compared with the classic essay in the central Italian section of

Berenson, B. *The Italian Painters of the Renaissance* (Phaidon, 1952).

And for the later Sienese painters, see

Pope-Hennessy, John. *Sienese Quattrocento Painting* (Phaidon, 1947).

There is a large literature on St. Catherine, some of it unreadable. The best introduction to her life is still probably

Gardner, E. *St. Catherine of Siena* (Dent, 1907).

More recent accounts include lives by

Curtayne, Miss A. (Sheed and Ward, 1929), and
Joergensen, J. (Longmans, Green and Co., 1938).

Ady, C. M. *Pius II* (Methuen, 1913), and
Memoirs of a Renaissance Pope (Allen and Unwin, 1960)

provide a good introduction to the life and times of Æneas Sylvius.

Two general books, of which the former is the more perceptive and has good illustrations, and the latter contains the fullest treatment of sacred pictures in out-of-the-way places, are

Colombier, P. du. *Sienna and Siennese Art* translated by Mary Fitton (Nicholas Kaye, 1957).

Hutton, E. *Siena and Southern Tuscany* (Hollis and Carter, 1910—new edition, 1955).

Burckhardt, T. *Siena, the City of the Virgin*, translated by M. Brown (O.U.P., 1960)

is generously illustrated and emphasises the religious aspect.

Sienese Chronology

Commune in existence 1125 or earlier	Hospital founded 1090	
Bishop expelled 1170		
Siena besieged by imperialists 1186		
Montalcino first taken 1202		
Wars with Florence 1205–08, 1229–35	Buonsignori bank founded 1209	
Grosseto first taken 1224	Duomo begun *c.* 1226	
Montepulciano first taken 1232		
THE TWENTY-FOUR 1233–70	*Palio* first mentioned 1238	
Wars with Florence 1251–54, 1256	University founded 1246	
Victory at Montaperti 1260		
Constitution 1262		
Defeat at Colle 1269	Nicola Pisano's pulpit 1269	
Guelf policy adopted 1270		Guido da Siena fl. 1260–80
Nobles excluded from power 1277		
	Giovanni Pisano's façade 1284–96	
THE NINE 1285 (1292)–1355		
Dante at San Gimignano 1300	(Papacy at Avignon 1309–76)	Duccio fl. 1278–1319, *Maestà* 1311
Talamone acquired 1303		
Constitution 1310	Palazzo Pubblico 1310	Simone Martini fl. 1315–44
Guidoriccio's campaign 1328	Torre di Mangia 1325–44	Lippo Memmi fl. 1317–56
Duke of Athens episode 1343	New Duomo attempted 1339–57	Pietro Lorenzetti fl. 1316–48
Black Death 1348		Ambrogio Lorenzetti fl. 1319–48
San Gimignano joins Florence 1353		
First visit of Charles IV 1355		
THE TWELVE 1355–68		
War with Perugia 1357–58		Barna fl. 1355–67
Company of the Hat defeated 1363	St. Catherine 1347–80	
Revolutions, Charles IV again 1368	to Avignon 1376	Andrea Vanni fl. 1355–1413
	(Great Schism 1378–1414)	Bartolo di Fredi fl. 1353–1410
THE RIFORMATORI (FIFTEEN) 1368–85		
League of the Caterpillar 1371	Duomo façade completed 1377	
	St. Bernardino 1380–1444	Sassetta fl. 1423–50
Siena under Giangaleazzo 1399–1404	Jacopo della Quercia fl. 1414–30	Sano di Pietro fl. 1428–81
Council of Siena 1423–24	Æneas Sylvius 1405–64	Giovanni di Paolo fl. 1425–82
Visit of Sigismund III 1432	to Scotland 1435	Domenico di Bartolo fl. 1428–47
Visit of Frederick III 1452	Pope Pius II 1458–64	Vecchietta fl. 1428–80
Victory at Poggio Imperiale 1479	Piccolomini palaces 1460–70	Matteo di Giovanni fl. 1460–95
Confused factional struggles 1480–96	Pienza rebuilt 1459–62	Francesco di Giorgio fl. 1465–1502
Rule of Pandolfo Petrucci 1497–1512		Neroccio fl. 1476–1500
Siena menaced by Cesare Borgia 1503	Marrina fl. 1500–17	
Liberty restored 1524	Sangallo at Montepulciano 1518–28	Pinturicchio's Library 1502–09
Victory at Porta Camollia 1526		Sodoma at Monte Oliveto 1505
Spanish garrison expelled 1552	Sir T. Hoby at Siena 1549–50	Beccafumi fl. 1512–51
Siege of Siena 1554–55		
Fall of government in exile at Montalcino 1559		

The Plates

1 The Campo from the Opera del Duomo

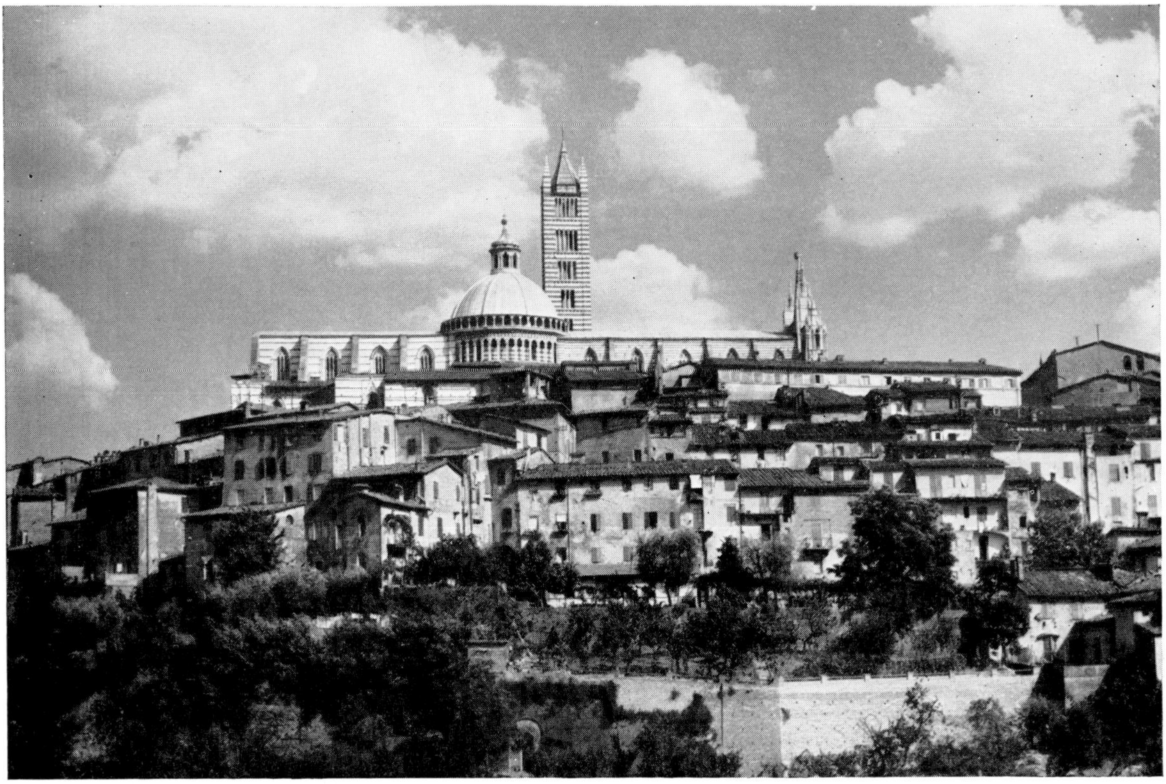

2 The Duomo from San Domenico

3 Fontebranda

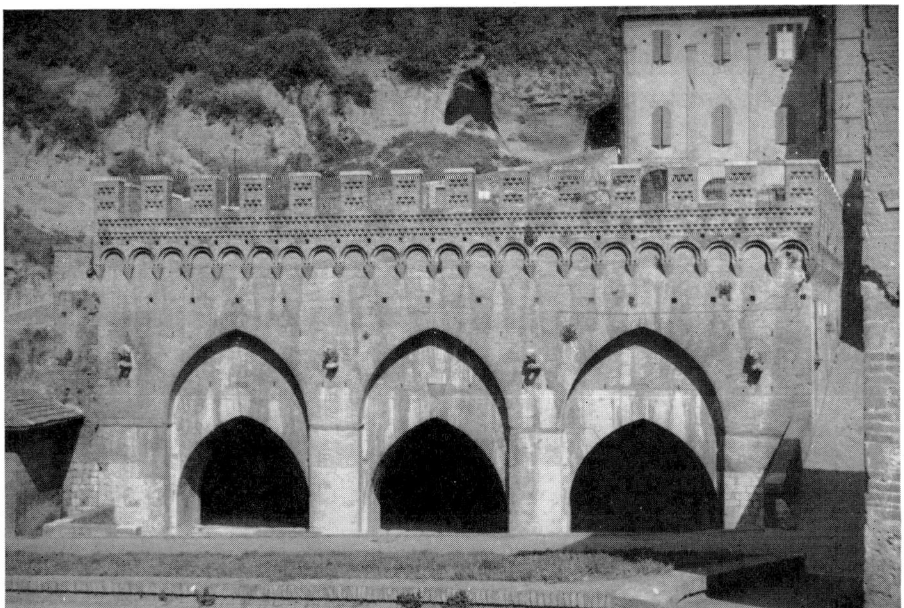

4 Early casa-torre in Via Stalloreggi

5 Palazzo Tolomei

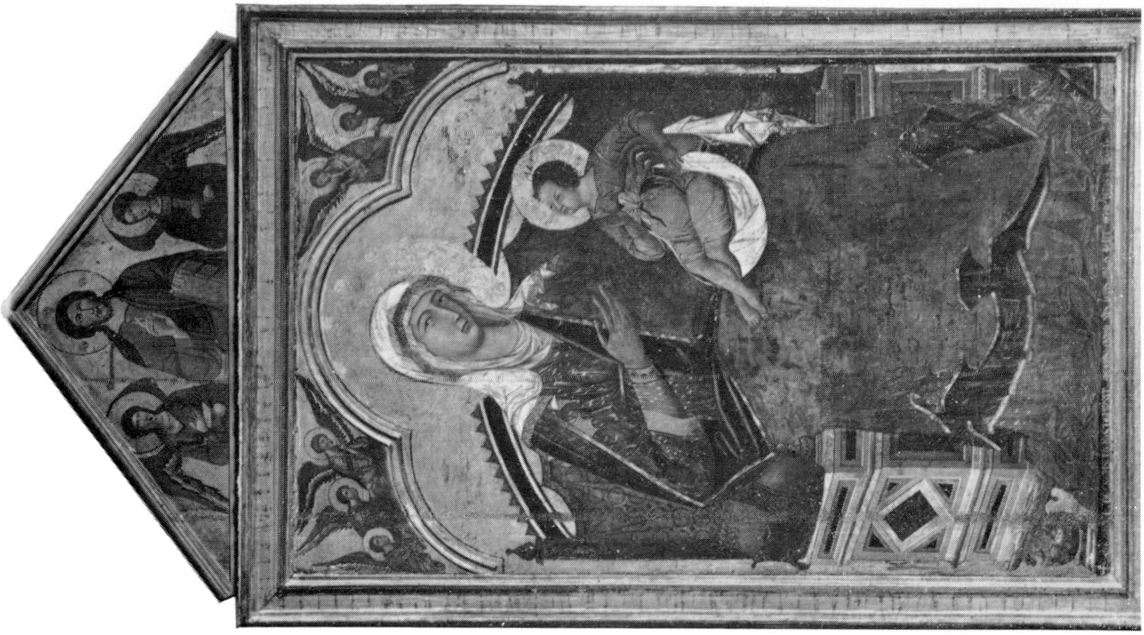

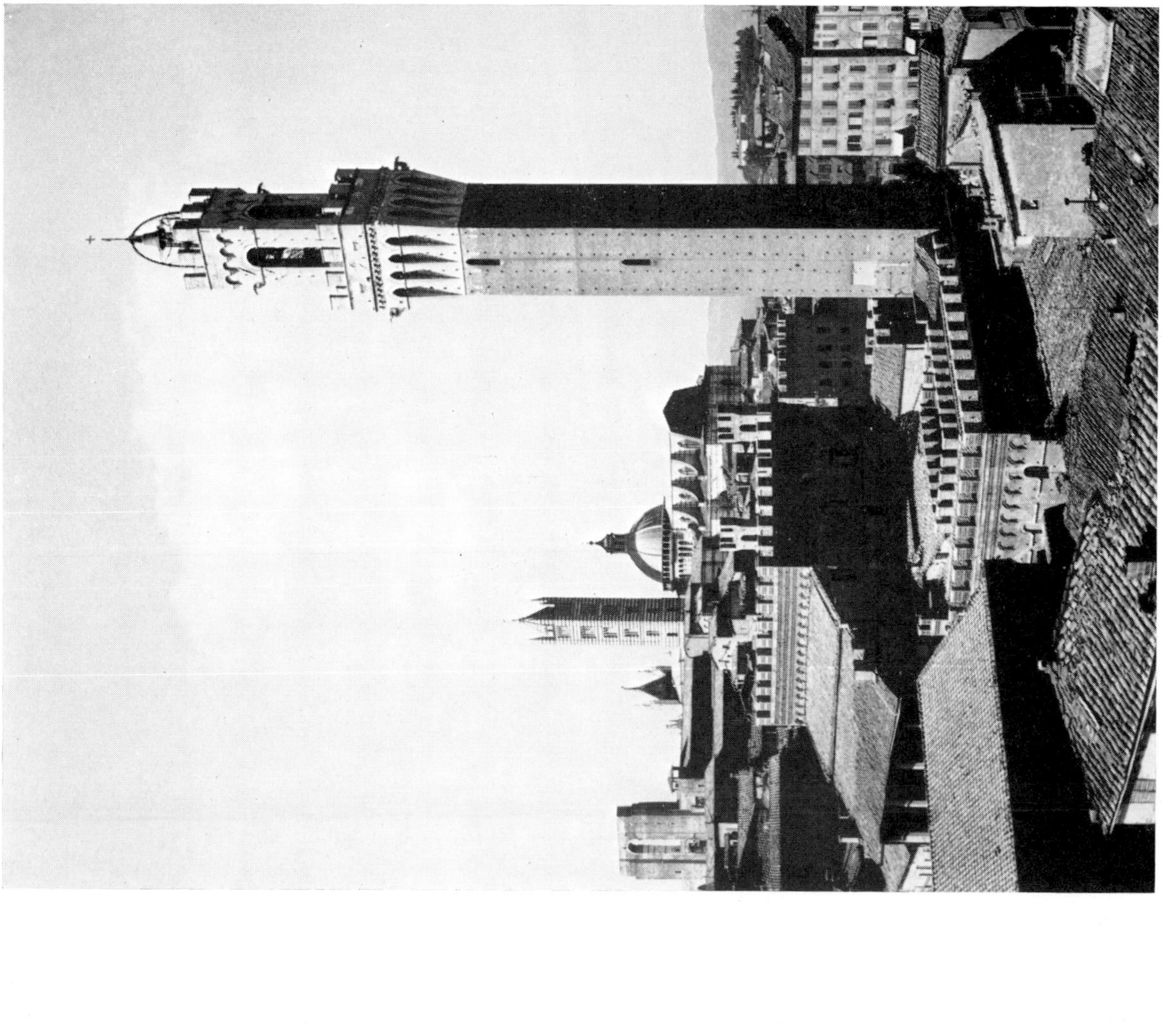

6 [*opposite*] Sienese skyline from San Martino

7 [*opposite*] Guido da Siena, Maestà

8 The Palio, from an eighteenth-century print

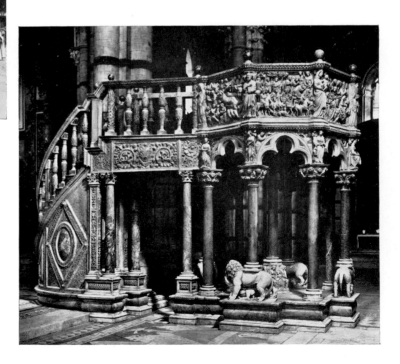

9 Standard-bearers of a contrada in the Campo

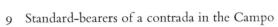

10 Nicola Pisano's pulpit

11 [*opposite*] The Duomo

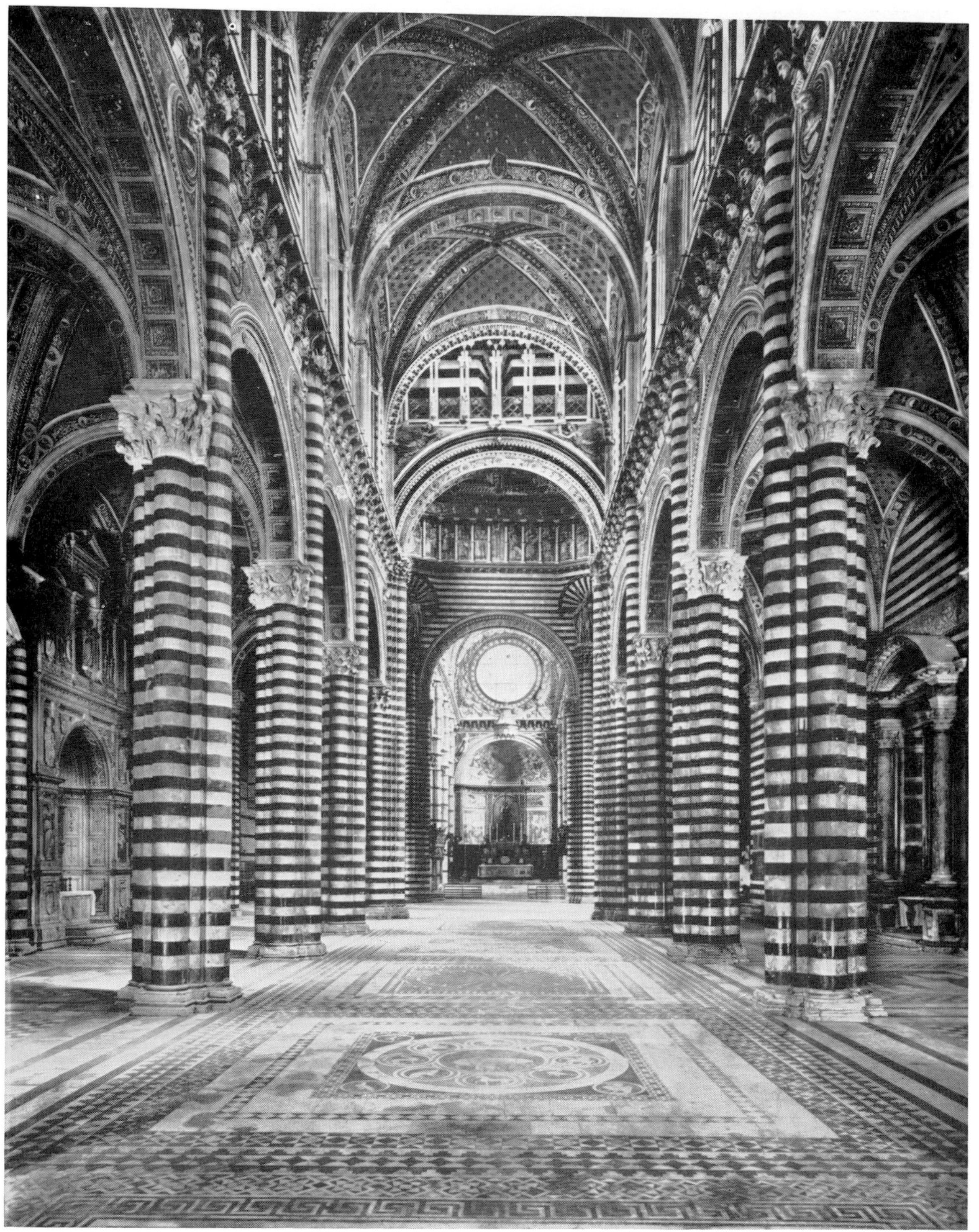

12 The Duomo, the nave

13 [*opposite*] Duccio, Madonna di Crevole

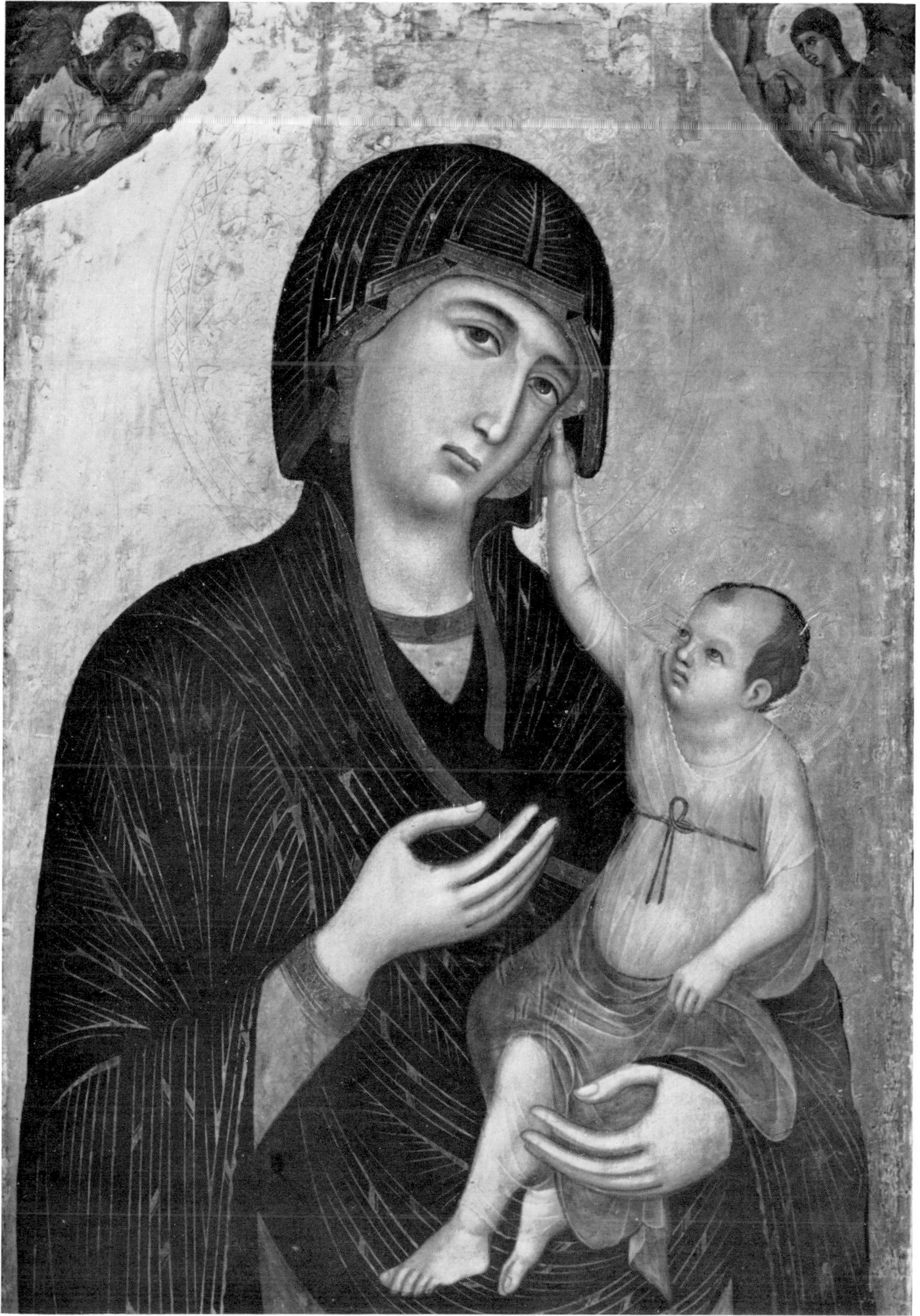

14 Duccio, head of an angel from the Maestà

15 Simone Martini, Agostino Novello's miracle

16 [*opposite*] Simone Martini, Guidoriccio

17 [*opposite*] Ambrogio Lorenzetti, Girls dancing (from Good Government)

ANO·DNI·MCCC·XX·VIII

18 Duccio, Maestà (as restored in 1960)

19 [*opposite*] Simone Martini, Maestà

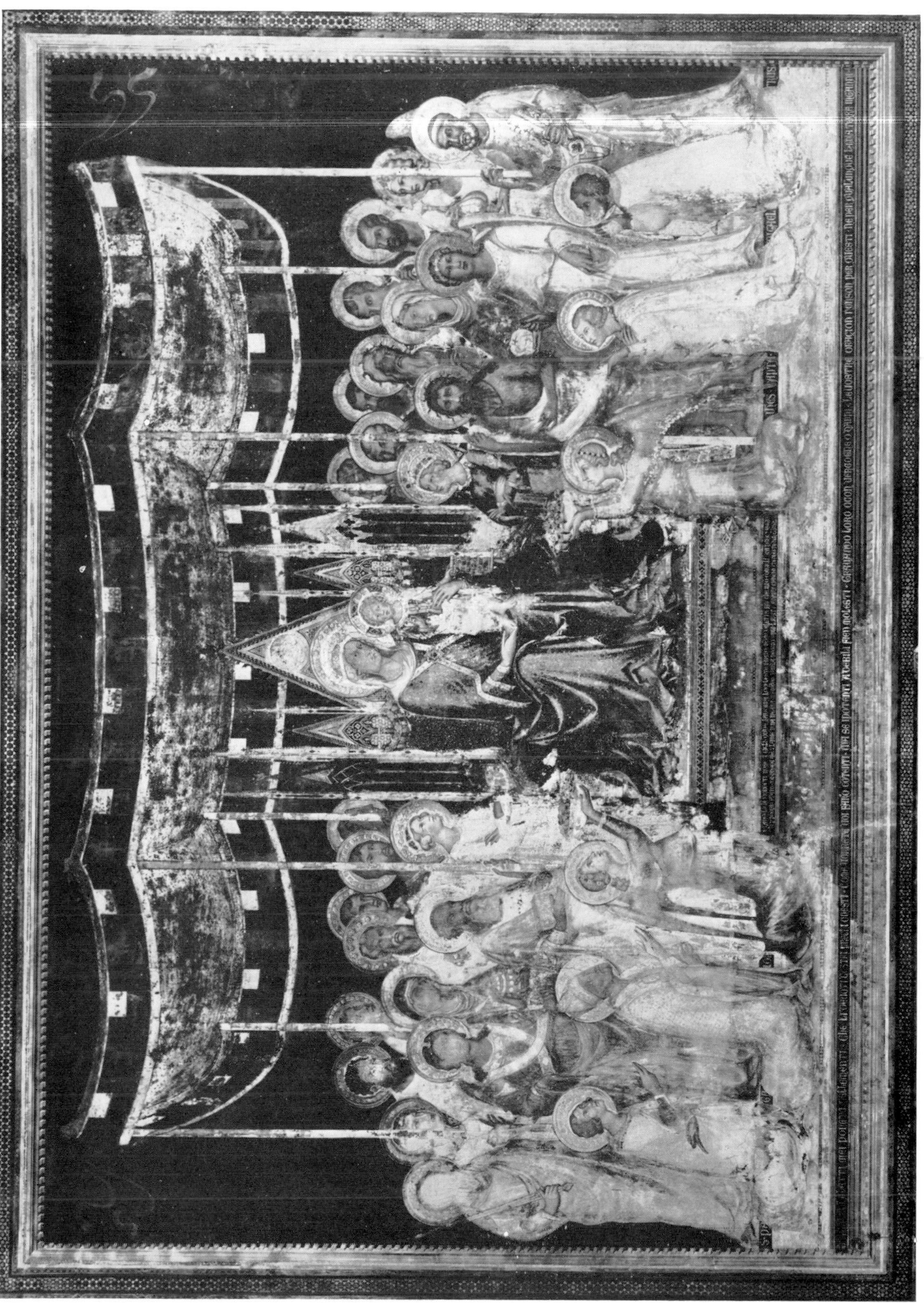

22 [*opposite*] Ambrogio Lorenzetti, Sienese councillors (from Good Government)

23 [*opposite*] Ambrogio Lorenzetti, Sienese coxcombs (from San Francesco)

20 Simone Martini, Madonna di Lucignano d'Arbia, before restoration

21 Simone Martini, Madonna di Lucignano d'Arbia, after restoration

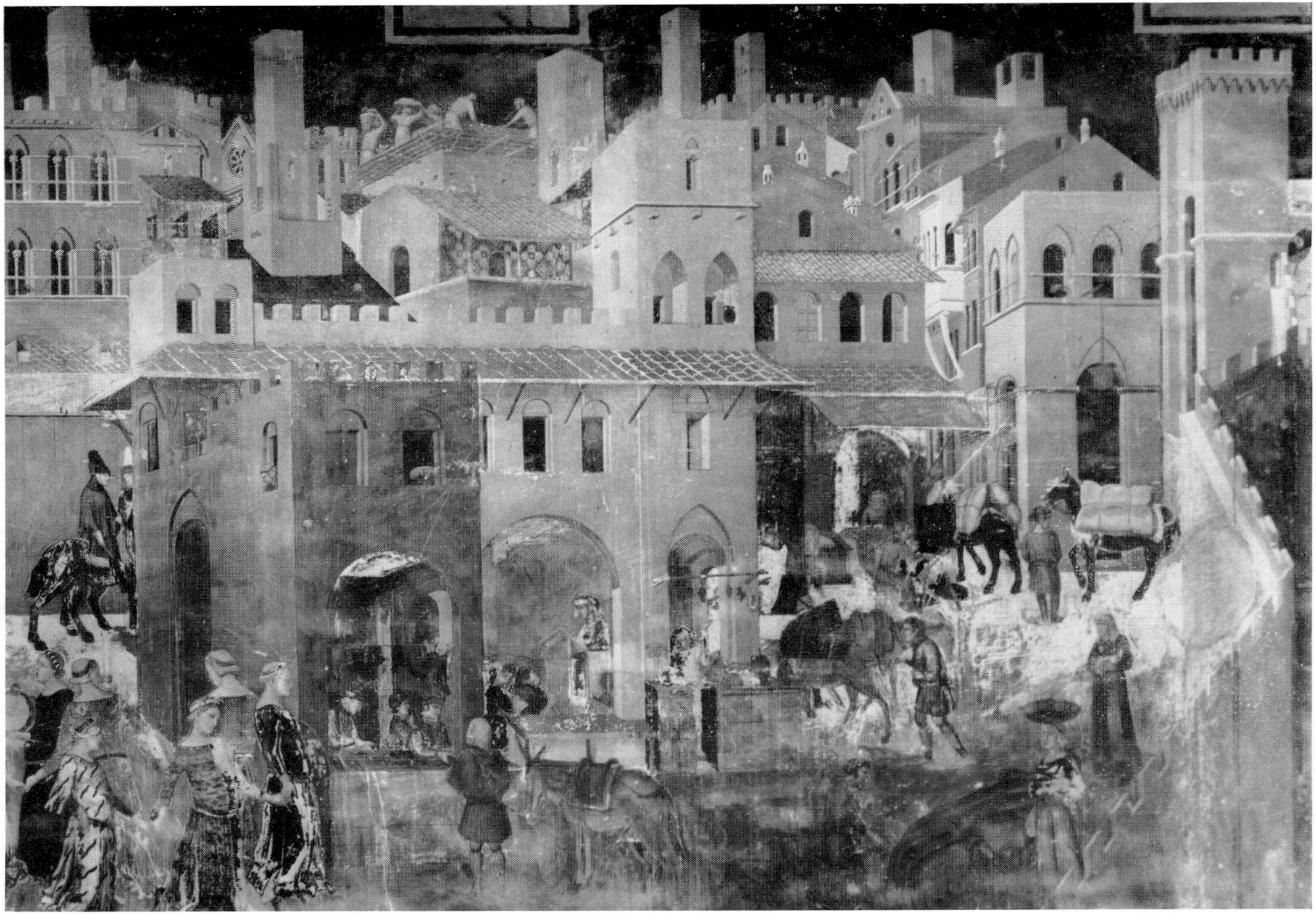

24 Ambrogio Lorenzetti, Good Government (inside the town)

25 [*opposite*] Ambrogio Lorenzetti, Good Government (outside the gate)

28 [*opposite*]
Palazzo Chigi-Saracini

26 Ambrogio Lorenzetti,
Madonna del Latte

27 Giovanni Pisano, head of
Miriam (taken from the
Duomo façade)

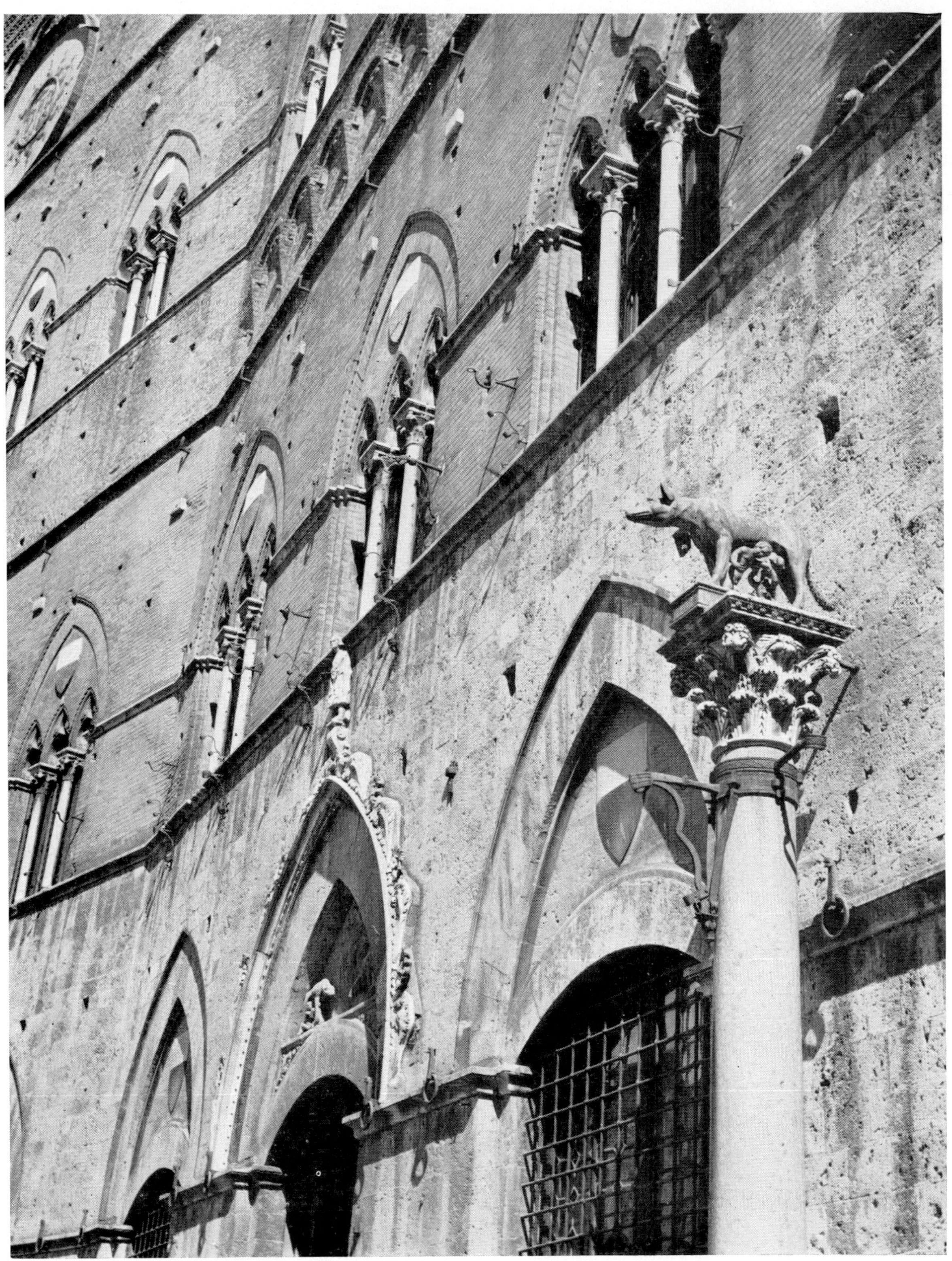

29 Façade of the Palazzo Pubblico

30 Arch and steps by the Baptistery

33 West front of the Duomo

31 [*opposite*] Domenico di Bartolo, Scene in the Hospital

32 [*opposite*] Neroccio, San Bernardino preaching in the Campo

36 [*opposite*] Neroccio, Madonna San Girolamo and San Bernardino

37 [*opposite*] Giovanni di Paolo, Madonna in a Landscape

34 Andrea Vanni, St. Catherine of Siena

35 Vecchietta, Pius II (detail from the Pienza Assumption)

38 Church of the Servi

39 Palazzo Piccolomini

40 Andrea Bregno, Piccolomini altar in the Duomo

43 [*opposite*] Pinturicchio, Frederick III meets his bride outside the Porta Camollia

41 Marrina, altar of the Fontegiusta church

42 Pinturicchio, Æneas Sylvius going to Basel

DE VM·MAXI
FE DI·VTRIS

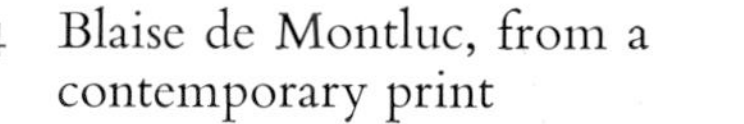

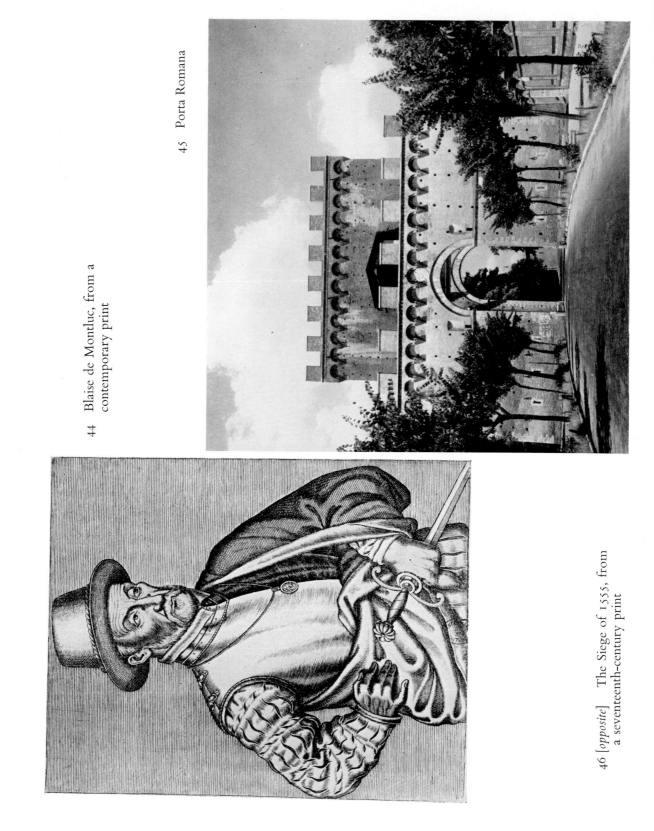

44 Blaise de Montluc, from a contemporary print

45 Porta Romana

46 [*opposite*] The Siege of 1555, from a seventeenth-century print

Il Vero ritratto della Citta di Siena con il sito di essa et forti di essa Citta e il Campo che
laßedia Intorno con iloro forti bordinij et baterie, alochi loro Justa et misurata.
Palazo de bondineli
Citadella
Spagnoli
bataglioni
Pogio di rauaciano

49 Monteriggioni, the 'diadem of towers'

50 The creta country

47 [*opposite*] Villa Paoletti (the Brownings' house)

48 [*opposite*] Cloister at Torri

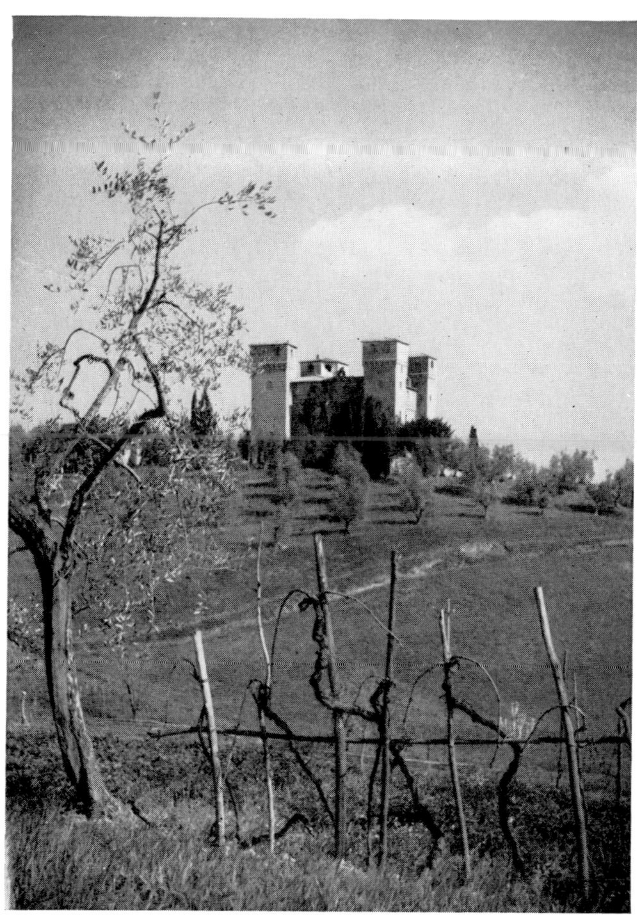

52 Quattro Torri

53 Landscape near Monte Oliveto

51 [*opposite*] Duccio, Madonna di Badia a Isola

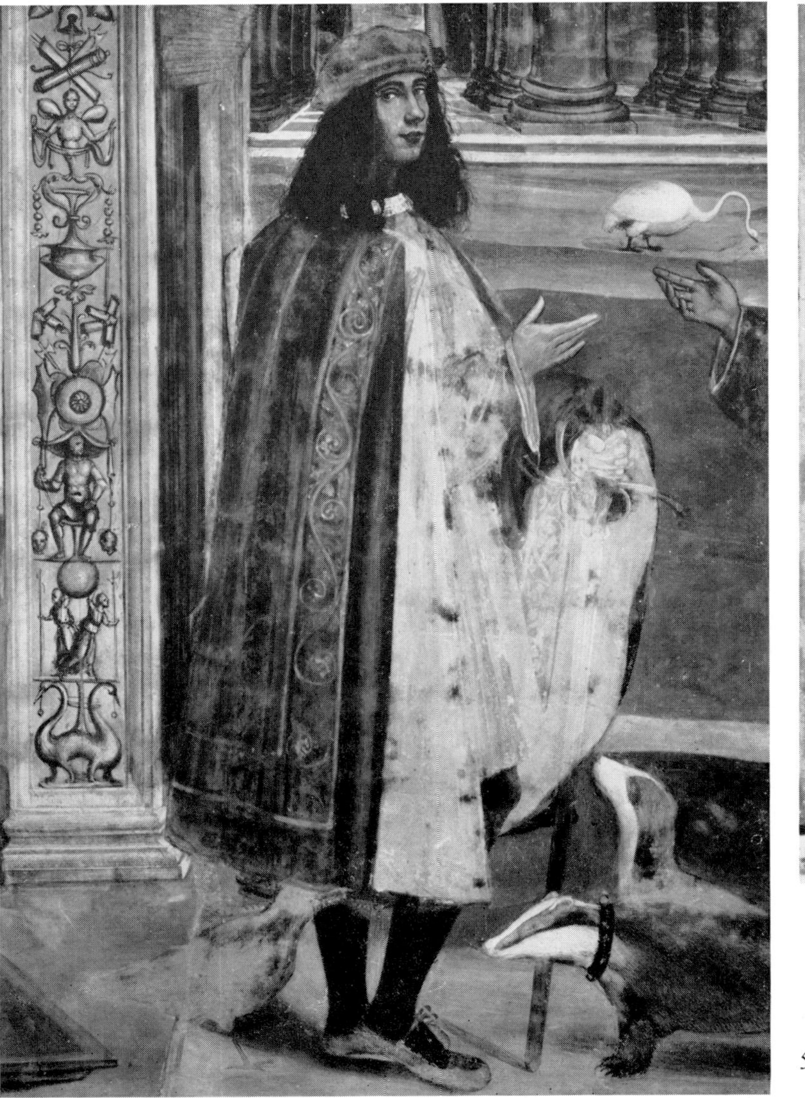

54 Sodoma, self-portrait with his badgers

55 Bartolo di Fredi, Job's banquet

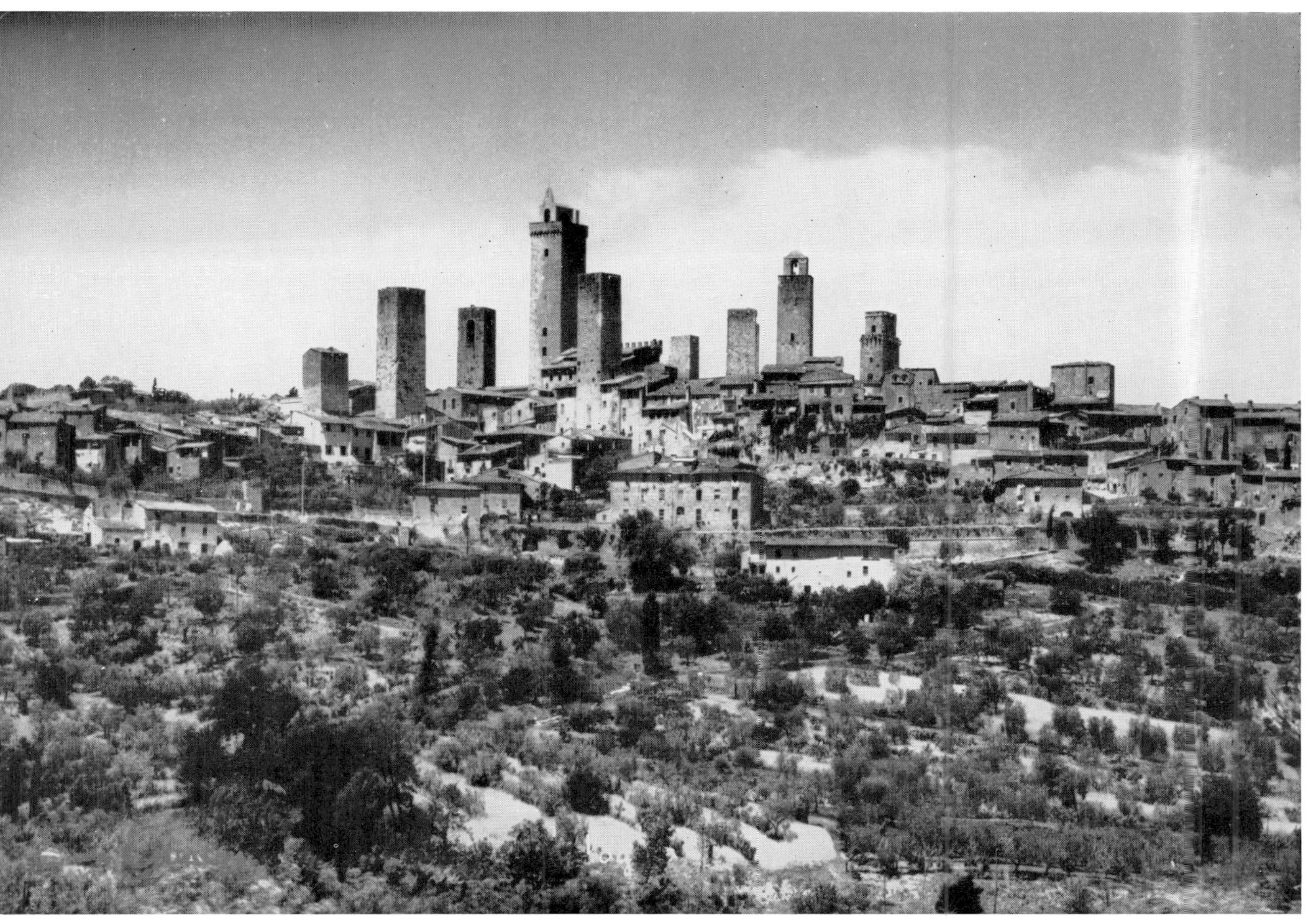

56 San Gimignano from the south-east

57 San Gimignano, towers from the Rocca

58 [*opposite*] Benozzo Gozzoli, St. Augustine's first day at school

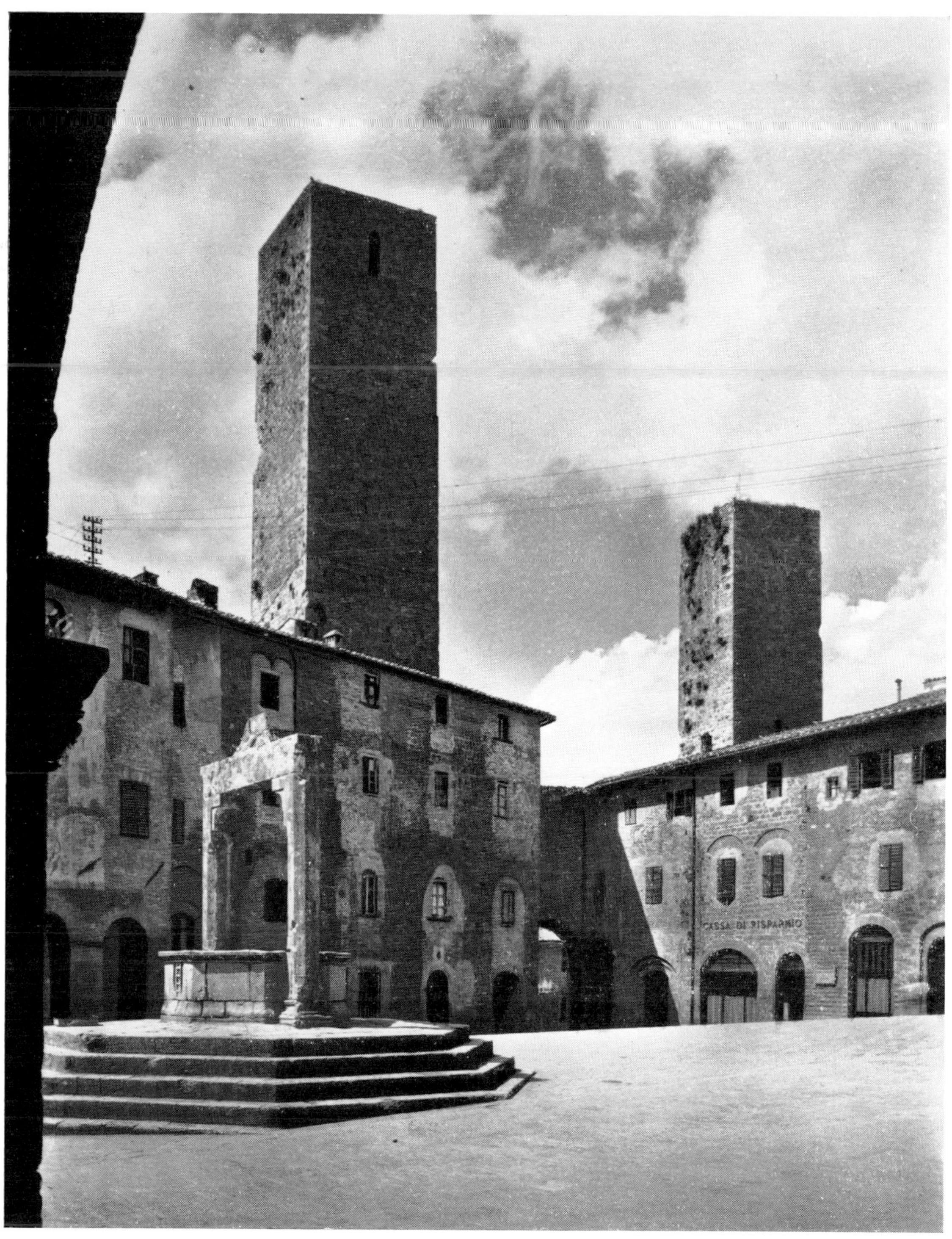

60 San Gimignano, Piazza Cisterna

59 [*opposite*] San Gimignano, Salvucci towers

61 Massa Marittima, cathedral

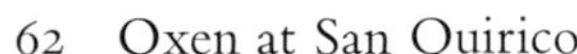

62 Oxen at San Quirico

63 Sant'Antimo

64 Pienza

65 Pienza, palazzo arcades from the garden

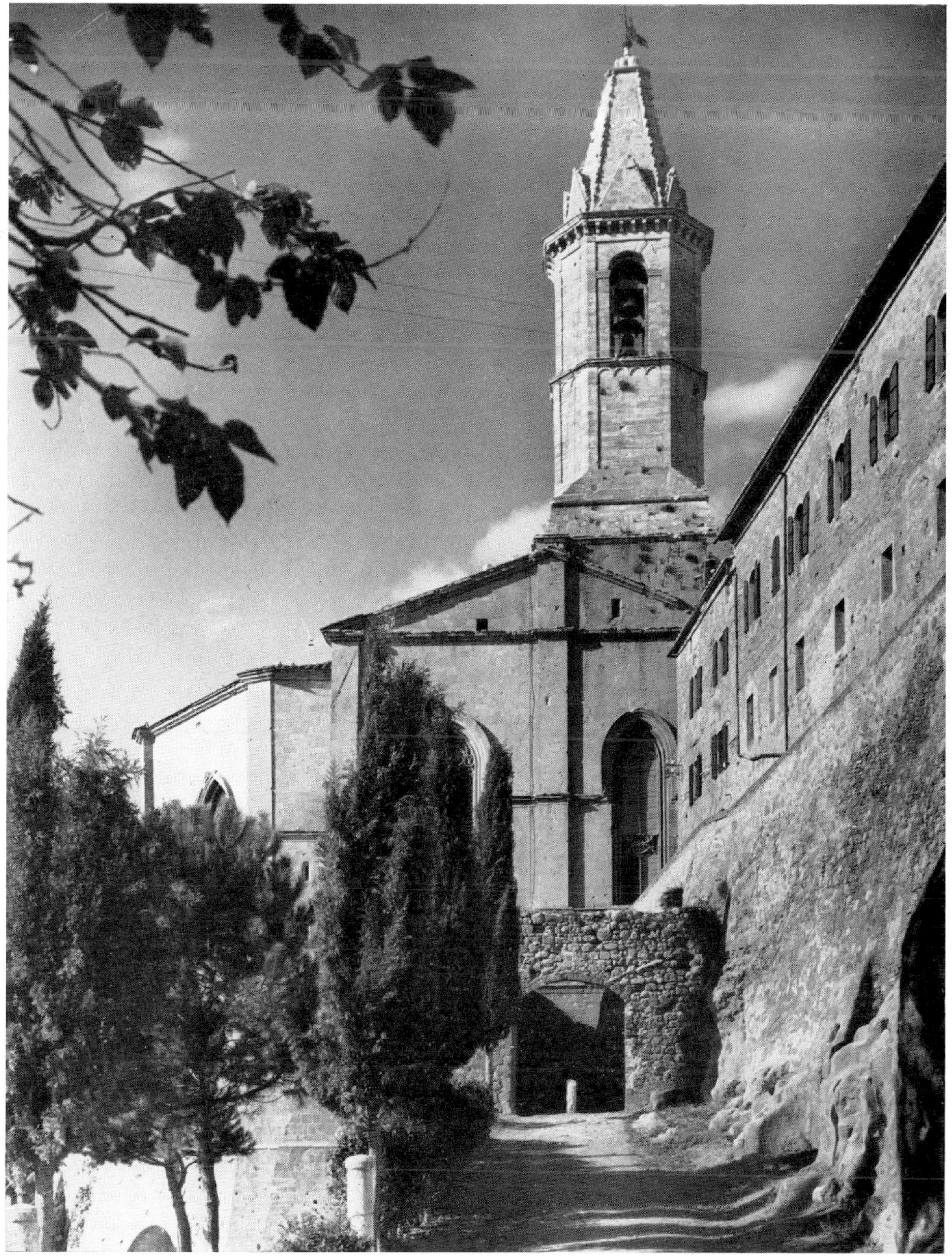

66 Pienza, postern gate

67 Pienza, the cathedral and palazzo

68 Montepulciano, Palazzo Tarugi

69 Montepulciano, well-head

70 Montepulciano, church of San Biagio

The Maps

THE SIENESE CONTADO

SIENA

N

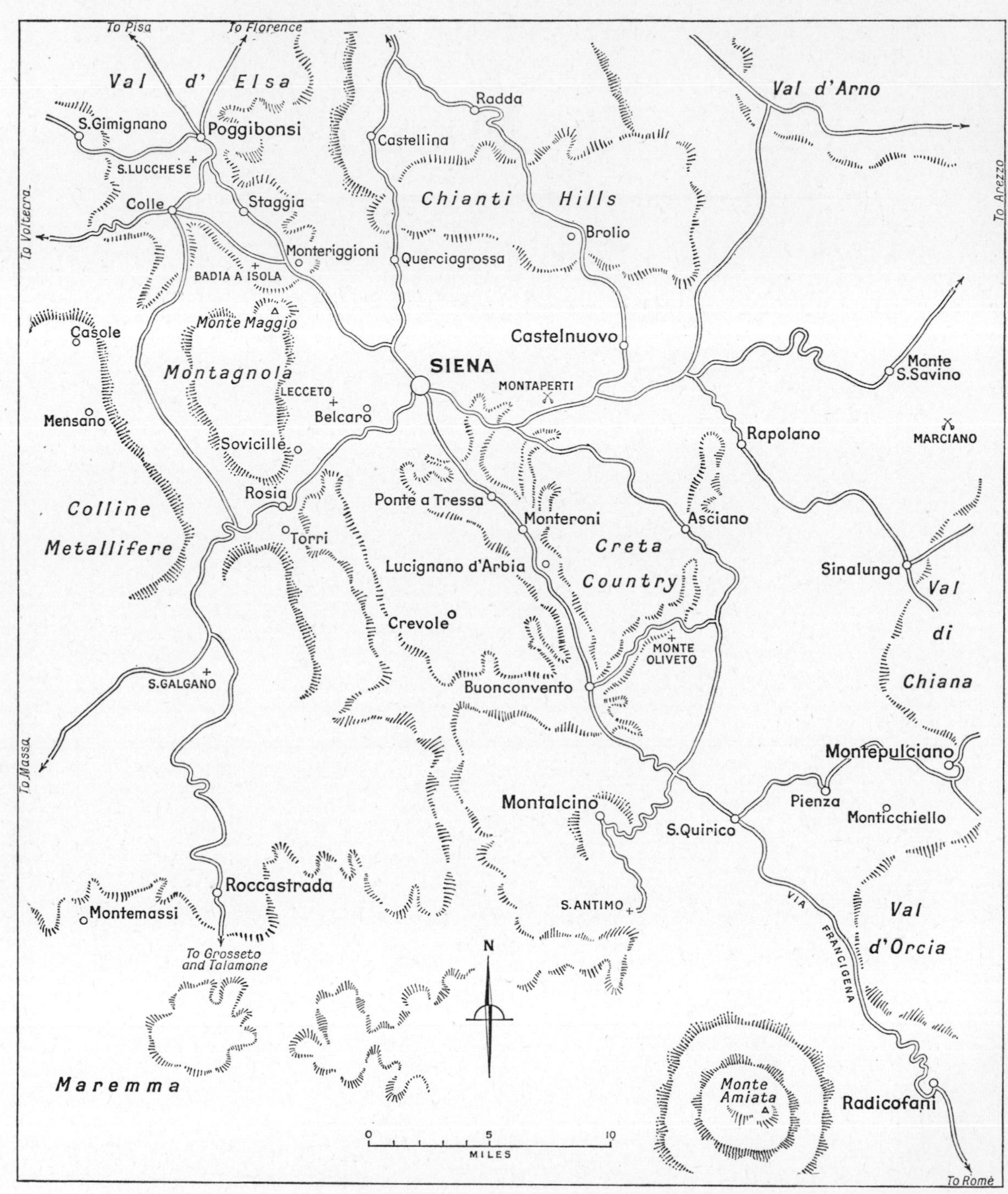

THE SIENESE CONTADO

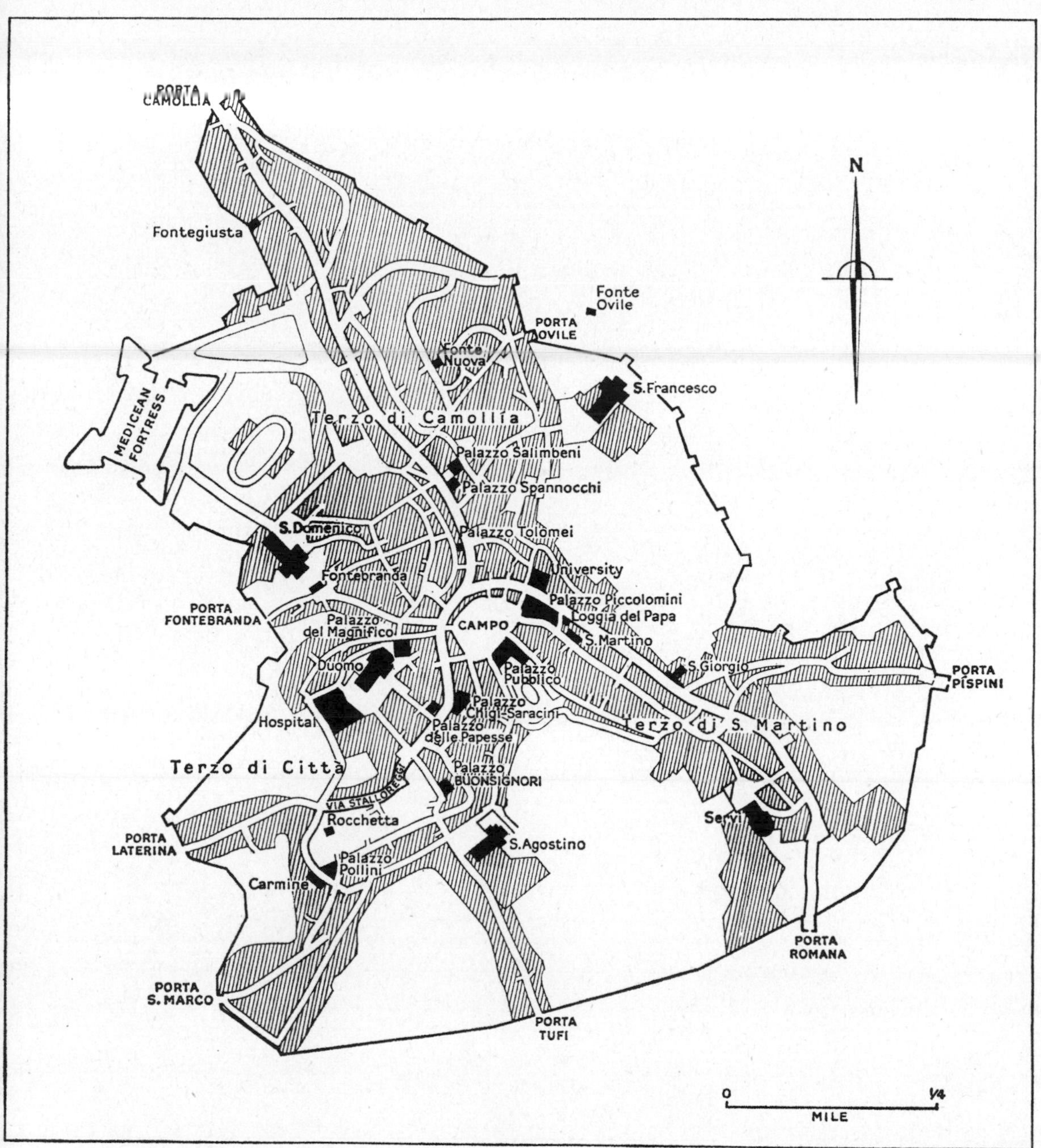
PORTA CAMOLLIA
Fontegiusta
N
Fonte Ovile
PORTA OVILE
Fonte Nuova
MEDICEAN FORTRESS
S.Francesco
Terzo di Camollía
Palazzo Salimbeni
Palazzo Spannocchi
S.Domenico
Palazzo Tolomei
Fontebranda
University
PORTA FONTEBRANDA
Palazzo Piccolomini
Loggia del Papa
Palazzo del Magnifico
CAMPO
S.Martino
Duomo
Palazzo Pubblico
S.Giorgio
PORTA PISPINI
Hospital
Palazzo Chigi-Saracini
Palazzo delle Papesse
Terzo di S. Martino
Terzo di Città
Palazzo BUONSIGNORI
VIA STALLOREGGI
Servi
Rocchetta
PORTA LATERINA
S.Agostino
Palazzo Pollini
Carmine
PORTA ROMANA
PORTA S. MARCO
PORTA TUFI
0
1/4
MILE

SIENA

Index

[Numerals in **bold** type refer to the numbers of the Plates]

Printed in Great Britain by Richard Clay and Company, Ltd.
Bungay, Suffolk